EVOLUTION OF INDIAN POLITY

EVOLUTION OF INDIAN POLITY

R. SHAMA SASTRI, B.A., M.R.A.S.

GYAN

Published by

GYAN

Gyan Publishing House
5, Ansari Road
Daryaganj, New Delhi-110002
Phone: 011-47034999, 9811692060
E-mail: books@gyanbooks.com

Distribution Network
gyanbooks.com
India, USA, Canada, UK, Australia, France

ISBN : 978-81-212-9634-2 (PB)
First Published, 1920

2nd Impression 2023

Printed at: Gyan Press, Delhi.

EVOLUTION OF INDIAN POLITY
Author: R. SHAMA SASTRI

EVOLUTION OF INDIAN POLITY

BY

R. SHAMA SASTRI, B.A., M.R.A.S.,
CURATOR, GOVERNMENT ORIENTAL LIBRARY, MYSORE,
PERIODICAL LECTURER IN POST-GRADUATE
CLASSES, CALCUTTA UNIVERSITY

1920

To

The Hon'ble Dr. Sir ASUTOSH MOOKERJEE,

Sarasvati, Sastra-Vachaspati, Sambuddhagama-Chakravarti,

Founder of Post-Graduate studies in the Calcutta University

which have been the most powerful academical incentive to original thought in India of Modern times,

the following pages are dedicated,

as an humble tribute of unbounded admiration for his Catholicity of heart and head knowing no limitations of colour, creed, or caste in welcoming knowledge from every quarter and in encouraging learning in the poorest cottages as well as in the proudest palaces,

by

the grateful Author.

न सन्ति दोषा विगुणा गुणा वा न सन्ति दोषानपहाय काव्ये ।
गुणाः प्रशास्तुः प्रभवन्तु कीर्त्यै पतन्तु दोषा मम मूर्ध्नि बाढम् ॥
इति प्रशास्त्रेऽत्र 'सर्' आशुतोषमुखार्यनाम्ने कृतिरर्पितेयम् ।
ततिस्स्रमानामिव निर्गुणाऽपि सदाशुतोषाय बुधाहृताऽस्तु ॥

TRANSLATION OF THE VERSES

In no work are there defects without merits or merits without defects. Let the merits be to the credit of the Inspirer; and let the defects heavily fall on my own head.

Thus this work, dedicated to the Inspirer, Sir Asutosh Mookerjee, may prove acceptable to the learned and for the pleasure of the good (for góod Asutosh) like a heap of flowers, though devoid of a string (quality).

PREFACE

This book contains the series of ten lectures delivered by me on the "Evolution of Indian Polity" under the Presidency of the Hon. Dr. Sir Asutosh Mookerjee, President of the Council of the Post-Graduate Studies in Arts at the Calcutta University in the months of March and April 1919. The first stage in the evolution, as detailed in the first lecture, is found universal and as such it requires no additional proof. The Institution of Elective Monarchy of Bachelor kings begotten by priests on a family of queens or cows as they are called, is peculiar to India; and no other nation has as yet been found to have passed through the institution of bachelor kings to hereditary monarchy which forms the third stage in the evolution of Indian polity. In all these stages, the monarchical element seems to have been under the powers of the Peoples' Assembly composed of priests, nobles (Râjas), traders and Agriculturists (Vis). As stated in the Mîmansa Sûtras of Jaimini, the king had no power over land, and was entitled only to $\frac{1}{6}$th of the produce.[1] Banishment or degradation of kings was one of the constitutional checks frequently employed for the prevention of the kings' extravagant proceedings and gambling and other vices.[2] The same constitutional check seems to have been employed even in the few Buddhist republics that prevailed side by side with monarchical institutions. What strikingly distinguishes India from the other contemporary nations in the application of such constitutional checks as banishment or degradation of tyrannical

---

[1] See Appendix C.

[2] Appendix A.

kings is its calm and peaceful procedure as contrasted with the bloody revolutions accompanied with horrible destruction of person and property in other nations. It is Atmamedha, also called prâyopaveśa or the vow of abstinence to death on the part of the people *en masse*[1] till the removal of the cause of their grievances.

The fourth stage in the evolution seems to have been the Damma-Chakka or Empire of Righteousness of the Jainas and the Buddhists. The rise of Jainism and Buddhism in India is not merely a religious revolt against the Brâhmanic animal sacrifices but an indirect and persuasive appeal to Vedic kings to abstain from their bloody warfare and animal sacrifices. Unlike the French revolution and the American War of Independence for man's rights of equality, fraternity and liberty, the directly religious and indirectly political propaganda of the Jainas and the Buddhists proclaiming equality and fraternity of men and charity to man and beast alike on the socio-political side, and control of passions and renunciation of the world for Nirvana or final emancipation on the spiritual side has with no destruction of property and person converted India into a peaceful Damma-Chakka or Empire of Righteousness and moral law on the ruins of old Brâhmanic Institutions, swept off the land together with their direct privileges and prerogatives. This Dhamma-Chakka is followed in its turn by the revival of old Dravidian monarchical institutions under the control of Brâhman priests and ministers and privileged castes, as desired by the politicians of the Kautilya period. The Andhras in Central India and the Pandyas, Cholas and Keralas in the South stood in as much need of the support of the Brâhmans for their revival as the latter in need of the support of the

---

[1] Appendix B.

Dravidians for the revival of their Vedic culture and institution. In the Vedic and Brâhmanic literature the Aryan monarch figured as a Kshatra or soldier paid for with bali or tax in the form of agricultural produce for protection of person and property of the people against enemies. In the Buddhistic literature he was Gana-dasa[1] or servant of the Buddhist Sangha fed by $\frac{1}{6}$th of the agricultural produce of the people. For his guilt, if any, he was liable to banishment, degradation or even the gallows. A monarch of such limited power could never be thought of as a reliable support of Brâhmanic culture just reviving or almost revived. The old Dravidians who had hitherto been regarded as Vrishalas or persons of Sûdra birth could scarcely afford shelter to Brâhmanic culture. It was therefore necessary to devise a new theory of monarchy and invest the Dravidian kings with the right of Sârvabhaumatva or power over all the land and people, as opposed to the old theory of the Mîmânsakas that the king has no right of ownership over land or people. A new theory of theocratic monarchy making the king's person divine and investing him with power over land and people in virtue of his building temples and setting up of idols of gods in the temples with rich endowments has been accordingly devised by the Bhatta school of the later Mîmânsakas (8th century onwards) and is thus stated in the first Dîdhiti of the Râjadharmakaustabha by Ananthadeva, son of Khandadeva, the author of Bhâttadîpika on the Mîmansa sûtras :—

"In the Śrîbhâgavatha the king is said to acquire his right of ownership of land of all kinds (Sarvaprakâra bhûmisvamya) only in virtue of his having set up idols of gods. 'He acquires ownership of all the land in virtue of

[1] P. 12, Ancient History of India by R. G. Bhandarkar.

his setting idols of gods, of the three worlds in virtue of his erecting a temple; of the abode of Brahma in virtue of his making endowments for the worship of gods; and he will attain equality with me (God Krishna) in virtue of his performances of the above three? Likewise in the Vishnudharmottara:—'Kings desirous of attaining to heaven should in the Kali age set up new cities after erecting temples.' Here the word cities implies villages and fortified towns also. The verse quoted from the Bhâgavata lays down that a king who is desirous of acquiring ownership of the cities, villages, towns and the like, which he establishes, should at first erect temples. Whoever is desirous of acquiring such ownership in virtue of his being anointed as a king shall also erect palace and other buildings at first. Hence it is that in enumerating the duties of a king, the erection of temples, palaces and the like are enumerated first. In the verse of the Bhâgavata the king is said to acquire his ownership of all the land in virtue of his setting up idols of gods and temples. In this connection there crop up two alternatives: whether the word 'mahîpâla,' 'king' in the verse means a person who is already exercising his royal duties as stated in the *primâ facie* view in the Jaimini's Mîmânsâ Sutra[1] or any other person of the ruling caste, as stated in the conclusion of the commentary on the same sutra? It cannot be the first meaning, for in that case there can be no necessity for the anointment of such a person. Nor is the erection of temple, etc., the duty of a person who is already exercising his royal duties, for his exercise of his royal duties is dependent on his acquisition of that power in virtue of his erection of temples or the like. Nor can it be the second, *i.e.*, any person of the ruling

[1] II. 3. 3.

caste, for in that case the construction of palaces and temples, etc., which can be undertaken by all, irrespective of caste and creed, would become a special duty of the Kshatriya caste. Not so; for though the erection of palaces and temples in general be undertaken by all, still, the construction of temples and palaces prior to the work of laying out cities, and villages can be regarded as a special duty of a person of Kshatriya caste in view of acquiring the right of sovereignty. In fact only such a person as is possessed of bravery, martial courage and other manly qualities befitting him to be a capable protector of people is taken as worthy of being anointed as a king. Hence like qualities such as bravery, courage, and capacity to protect, the construction of temples and other buildings befits a person to be a sovereign of the people."

There is no doubt that this new theory of theocratic monarchy was universally accepted in India in mediaeval period. The existence of a great number of temples in the ruined capitals of ancient kings in India, especially in the Dekhan, proves it beyond doubt. It has been usual with historians to regard this form of monarchy as despotic. But I doubt whether the temple-builders of the mediaeval period were so despotic as they were believed to have been. As a matter of fact effective religious restraint and priestly domination seem to have been the characteristic features of Indian monarchies in general, and of mediaeval states in special. With this last step ends the evolution of Indian polity, having its growth arrested by Mahamadan conquest of India in the North, while in the South a number of Hindu kings vied with each other in establishing their sovereign rights by studding the land with temples. It is true that we regret to miss such sweet and bewitching words as Equality, Fraternity, Liberty,

Self-determination and the like in the political history of India. Yet I am inclined to believe that such religious and moral restrain's as Self-denial, Conquest of the Six Passions, Preparation for Moksha or Nirvana by renunciation frequently preached to the prince and the poor alike were scarcely less powerful than the constitutional and legal checks of Western nations of modern times. How far the modern constitutional checks based more on utilitarian than ethical principles are preferable to religious or philosophical restraints which are applicable to all is a question yet to be decided.

I shall be guilty of ingratitude if I close the preface without acknowledging my thankfulness to Sir Asutosh Mookerjee, the President and Founder of Post-Graduate Studies in Arts in the Calcutta University, for his kind invitation to me at a great distance from Calcutta to read a series of lectures on subjects connected with the Arthasastra in that Institution which is unique and the only one of its kind in India. I confess that in my naturally ready response to his generous invitation, I have fallen far short of what was expected of me as the discoverer and translator of the Kautiliya Arthasastra. For this I beg to apologize to the worthy President of the Council of Post-Graduate Studies as well as to the world of scholars at large. My thanks are also due to the Senate of the Calcutta University for the publication of my lectures.

MYSORE,
The 10th September, 1920. R. S.

CONTENTS

EVOLUTION OF INDIAN POLITY

LECTURE I

TRIBAL STATE OF SOCIETY

It is chiefly to woman that man owes his civilisation. Such of her natural qualities as sweetness, beauty and love seem to have infused or awakened in him the qualities that are necessary for sociability. Taking advantage of the natural feeling of love which man has for woman, she seems to have brought him under her influence and taught him the art of extending that love first towards her own children and next to her distant blood-relations. While this is as much true of beasts and birds, the difference between beasts and birds on the one hand and man on the other lies in his retentive memory and his natural capacity to repeat in word and action the impressions made on his memory. This natural gift of memory and tongue would have enabled him to evolve under the influence of woman knowingly or unknowingly a kind of society congenial for the exercise of his natural talents. But the brute force which man has in common with beasts to acquire and carry off the object of his liking, whether woman or food, seems to have disturbed him very much in his conscious or unconscious attempt to live a social life with his woman or women and children. In the early stages of society man like a beast seems to have fought with man for woman or food.

This kind of herd life seems to be as true of human society in its earliest stages as of beasts even now. It needs no proof that if human society once existed in such a rude and undeveloped form as this, it was in that stage maternal or matriarchical rather than paternal or patriarchical. At this stage of society it was not possible for children to recognise their father as easily as their mother who sucked, protected, and maintained them. The proof for this lies in the fact that children once went by their mother's name instead of by their father's name, a practice quite opposite to what now prevails. Words such as Daityas, sons of Diti, Vainateyas, sons of Vinatâ, Kâdraveyas, sons of Kadrû, Anjaneya, son of Anjanâ, Jâbala, son of Jâbalâ, and Jaratkâra, son of Jaratkâru are taken as indicative of the uncertainty of the real begetter and of the unsettled condition of the society which rendered promiscuity among women a necessary evil.[1] The Lâtyâyana Srauta Sûtra and the Nidâna Sûtra of the Sâma Veda furnish a still more reliable proof of promiscuity of early women than this. In I. 3, 17-19 the Lâtyâyana Srauta lays down that in Agnishtoma Sattra and other sacrifices the Subrahmanya priest should, while singing the Subrahmanya litany enumerate the names of the father, grandfather, and great-grand-father as well as of the son, grandson, and great-grand-son of the sacrificer. After inquiring after the reason for the enumeration of such names, the Nidâna Sutra (III. 8) says as follows :—

"Women are of disorderly conduct. He, the sacrificer, here before divine and human witnesses, declares after mounting the sacrificial car the names of those whose descendant he is as well as the names of those whom he

---

[1] Ency. Brit., Vol. IX, pp. 20-25.

calls his own descendants, lest King Soma may mount his car (and not come down)."

The Mahabharata furnishes a still clearer proof of this in the legend of Svetaketu (Adiparva, Chapter 128, Kumbhakona Edition) :—

" Formerly women were not confined in their houses and dependent on husbands and other relatives. They used to go about freely enjoying as best pleased them. They did not then adhere to their husbands faithfully and yet they were not regarded sinful, for that was the sanctioned custom of the times. That very custom is followed to this day by birds and beasts without any exhibition of jealousy. That practice, sanctioned by precedent, is applauded by great Rishis. The practice is yet regarded with respect amongst the Northern Kurus. Indeed, that custom, so lenient to women, has the sanction of antiquity. The present practice (of woman being confined to one husband for life) has been established but lately. I shall tell thee now in detail who established it and why. It has been heard by us that there was a great Rishi named Uddalaka. He had a son called Svetaketu who was also an ascetic of merit. The present virtuous practice was established by that Svetaketu in anger. Hear thou the reason for his anger. One day, in the presence of Svetaketu's father, a Brahmana came and holding Svetaketu's mother by the hand, told her—' Let us go.' Beholding his mother seized by the hand and taken away apparently by force, the son, moved by wrath, became very indignant. Seeing his son indignant Uddalaka addressed him and said,—" Be not angry, O Son ! This is the practice sanctioned by antiquity. Women of all orders in this world are free. Just as cattle are situated so are human beings, too, within their respective orders. Svetaketu, however, disapproved of this custom and established in the world the present practice both for men and women.

The conversation of Gautama with Satyakama Jabala about the uncertainty of the latter's parentage, as narrated in Chhandogya, IV. 4, 5, is another instance pointing to the same conclusion.

I shall have occasion to speak, in connection with the origin of Kshatriyas, of a Vedic institution of queens or cows with no marriage tie, a custom on which the peculiar custom of the Nairs of Malabar seems to have been founded. Among the Nairs the woman lives with her mother or brother or in other cases has a house of her own where she receives her husband. "No Nair knows his father, and every man looks upon his sister's children as his heirs." (Buchunan, II. 412).

These are strong evidences to prove that the family system among the Aryans of India or among their predecessors was of yore rather maternal or matriarchical than paternal or patriarchical and that it was due to the inability of woman to defend herself against her ravisher and a peculiar kind of moral sense on the part of men.

From this licentious or dissolute state of society in which safety of person and property was out of question, the next step in the evolution of society seems to have been the formation of a defensive and offensive union of men and women as a protective measure. A number of settlements or unions of men and women seems to have arisen in various places under a common appellation, Gaṇa, Jana, or Kula. Each Gaṇa or Jana seems to have adopted a different badge or banner of an animal, plant, or bird as its distinguishing mark, and as a device showing the superiority or inferiority in bravery of one Gaṇa to the other. It is a strange coincidence that though widely separated from each other, different communities or tribes of men appear to have adopted similar badges or totems as they are termed by ethnographers. The totem names of the North American tribes of Senecas are said to be wolf, bear, turtle, beaver, deer, snipe, heron, and hawk. The same names are said to prevail among other tribes known as Cayygas, Oneidas, Mohawks, and the rest.[2] The totem names that seem to have once prevailed among the Aryans of India are horse, elephant, goat, serpent, dog, cat, rat, cow, buffalo, tiger, deer, monkey, lion, mungoose, eagle, owl, crow, cock, peacock, banner, smoke, lion, dog, bull, ass, elephant, and the like.

There is reliable evidence to prove that the early Aryans were divided into as many tribes as are indicated by the names of the beasts, birds, and other objects mentioned above. It is an immemorial custom with the Hindus generally that the suitability of a proposed marriage match should be based upon day, gens, and other astrological harmonies between the bride and the bridegroom. There are as many as twenty harmonies or Kûṭas, as they are called, to be ascertained, before the selection of a bride or bridegroom is declared acceptable. The most historically though not astrologically important Kûṭas or harmonies are the (1) Gaṇakûṭa, or tribe-harmony, (2) the Yonikûṭa or species-harmony, (3) the Pakshikûṭa or bird-harmony, (4) the Bhutakûṭa or elements harmony, (5) Ayakûṭa or prosperity harmony, (6) Varnakûṭa or class or caste harmony, and (7) Gotrakûṭa or family harmony. The way in which these harmonies are to be found out is thus explained in the Kâlâmrita (Chapter III).

Of the 27 stars, some nine stars are assigned to Devagaṇas or celestial tribes, some other nine to Rakshasagaṇas or demon tribes, and the remaining nine to human

---

[2] Ency. Brit., Vol. IX, p. 20.

tribes. It is ruled that if both the bride and the bridegroom have birth-stars belonging to the same tribe, they are said to have Gaṇa-harmony. These birth-stars should never belong to inimical tribes such as demoniac and human, in which case the proposed match should be given up.

The Yonikûṭa or species-harmony is thus explained :—

The species are taken to be fourteen :—(1) horse, (2) elephant, (3) goat, (4) serpent, (5) dog, (6) cat, (7) rat, (8) cow, (9) buffalo, (10) tiger, (11) deer, (12) monkey, (13) lion, (14) mungoose. These together with their females are made 28. Of the 27 stars, made into 28 with the addition of the Abhijit, one star is assigned to each of the 28 species, male and female. It is ruled out that the couple should have their birth-stars belonging to the same species or such different species as are not naturally inimical to each other.

Similarly to each of the five birds such as, eagle, owl, crow, cock, and peacock, some five and five stars are assigned and to the second and third bird one more star is also assigned to make up 27. If the couple are found to have such birth-stars as are assigned to the same bird, they are said have bird-harmony.

Likewise the 27 stars are distinguished among the so-called five elements, earth, air, water, fire and ether. It is ruled that the birth-stars of the couple should belong to the same or friendly elements, but never to inimical elements.

To find out Ayakûṭa or prosperity-harmony, the astrologer is directed to proceed as follows :—

The eight cardinal points, East, South-East, South, South-West, West, North-West, North and North-East are designated by the names, flag, smoke, lion, dog, bull, ass, elephant and crow. Out of the 27 stars, three, three stars are assigned to each of the cardinal points and the remaining three stars are added to the first three points, one to each, thus making up 27. The points with their names being marked on the circumference of a circle, the fifth point, counting from any initial point, is considered to be the enemy of the first. The birth-stars of the couple are considered to be in harmony, if they do not belong to inimical points.

The class or caste-harmony is thus explained :—

Some three zodiacal signs are assigned to Brahman class, some three to Kshatriya class, some three to Vaisya and the remaining three to Sudra. If the birth signs of the bride and bridegroom are of the same class or if that of the bridegroom is of higher class than that of the bride, they are said to be in class-harmony.

The Gotra or family harmony is explained as follows :—

The progenitors of families are said to be seven : Marichi, Atri, Vasishtha, Angiras, Pulastya, Pulaha and Kratu. The 28 stars with Abhijit are distributed among the 7 progenitors at 4 stars to each. The couple are said to be in family harmony, if their birth-stars belong to different families.

Mere totemism in a good sense and astrology appear to be so inseparably mixed up that it is hardly possible to find out which gave the lead to the other. But as such totemic names, if they are totemic at all, are found among savage tribes of other nations with no connection with stars or zodiacal signs, it stands to reason to hold that they are of totemic origin, intended to sanction or prohibit marriage between persons of the same totem name and to acknowledge the duty to support in war or to revenge other members of the same name. And as civilization advanced and as tribes of different totems became amalgamated together by conquest or reconciliation, such totem names as a cat-man, a rat-maid, might have still persisted in the retentive recollection of old men and women and might have led a shrewd astrologer to explain the totem name by connecting it with the birth date or birth star of the persons. That stars, days, months and hours of the day were of old designated by names of animals, plants, and other things, is clearly borne out by history.[3] Thus there is reason to believe that though Kâlâmrita and other astronomical treatises are of recent date, still the totem names recorded in them are of prehistoric origin, traditionally handed down from generation to generation. Accordingly even in the Vedas mention seems to have been made of such totem names as 'Sigru, horse-radish, and aja, goat'[4] in connection with tribes. The way in which the sacrificer is directed in the Krishnayajurveda (VI. 6, 4, 17) to assign to the twelfth stake his enemy or a rat seems to imply the tendency of the times to designate a hostile tribe by the name, rat. The names of the eleven sacrificial animals, enumerated in the Krishnayajurveda (V. 5, 11, 49) may have some remote connection with totemic custom. Side by side with this regulation of marriages by totem names, as set forth in the first five harmonies mentioned above, there is also the institution of gotras or families on patriarchical basis, prohibiting the marriage of a woman of the same gotra, as well as of a woman descended from his paternal or maternal ancestors within the sixth degree.

Now the question is how these two customs of marriage, one based upon rational maternal family system and regulated by totem names of tribes, and the other connected with families established on patriarchical basis and indicative of an advanced form of society, are to be reconciled with each other. The answer is furnished by

[3] Ency. Brit., Vol. XXIV, p. 793.

[4] Rigveda, VII. 18, 19.

a guiding astrological verse commonly quoted by astrologers. It is as follows :—

"Friendship between the lords of the birth-signs of the bride and bridegroom is essential among the Brahmans; regulation of marriage by gaṇa-harmony (as explained above) is essential among the Kshatriyas; the distance of the birth-stars of the bride from that of the bridegroom (by about 180°) is important for the Vaisyas; species-harmony (as explained above) is essential for the Sudras."[5]

From this it can be safely inferred that the Sudras, a race different from the Aryans, were divided into a number of totemic tribes at war with each other and with families organised on maternal basis. It is probable that when they were taken into the Aryan fold rather by reconciliation than by sword by the invading Aryans, the latter had incorporated with their own many of their former's religious, social and political customs and that promiscuity of women, regulation of marriage by totemic names, and Niyoga or the custom of deputing a man to beget a son on an appointed wife were customs rather of the Sudras than of the Aryans. What were the other religious, social, and political customs of the Sudras which the Aryans had incorporated with their own is a question that seems to be a rich mine for explorers. Leaving this knotty question aside, it may, however, be presumed that when the Aryans invaded, India they consisted of families organised on a patriarchical basis, as vividly described by the following soul-stirring hymn of the Atharva-veda (III. 30) :—

"Freedom from hate I bring to you, concord and unanimity.

---

[5] See Kâlâmrita, Chapter 3, verse 139.

1. Love one another as the cow loveth the calf that she hath borne.

2. One-minded with his mother let the son be loyal to his sire. Let the wife, calm and gentle, speak words sweet as honey to her lord.

3. No brother hate his brother, no sister to sister be unkind. Unanimous, with one intent, speak ye your speech in friendliness.

4. That spell through which gods sever not, nor ever bear each other hate.

That spell we lay upon your home, a bond of union for the men.

5. Intelligent, submissive, rest united, friendly and kind, bearing the yoke together.

Come speaking sweetly each one to the other. I make you one-intentioned and one-minded.

6. Let what drink, your share of food be common, together with one common bond I bind you.

Serve Agni, gathered round him like the spokes about the chariot nave.

7. With binding charm I make you all united, obeying one sole leader and one-minded. Even as the gods who watch and guard the Amrit at morn and eve may ye be kindly-hearted."

There is also philological evidence to prove that before the Aryans of India had separated from their brethren, the Greeks, the Romans, the Celts and others, they had arrived at a state of society in which families on a constitutional basis were firmly set up. The following list of words common to the three kindred languages Sanskrit, Greek and Latin, is a suitable evidence of the formation of families on patriarchical basis and of a tribal or democratic form of Government :—

Sanskrit.	Greek.	Latin.	English.
pitar	pater	pater	father
matar	mater	mater	mother
bhratar	phratria	frater	brother
naptar	anepsios	nepos	grandson
jamatar	gambros	gener	son-in-law
svasura	becura	gocer	father-in-law
widhava		vidua	widow
rajan		rex	king
rajni		regina	queen
patni	posis	potens	mistress honourable
padati	pezos	peditis	footman
rajata	arguros	argentum	silver
dama	domos	domos	house
vis or vesa	foikos	vicus	house, village
pur	polis		city
nau	nans	navis	ship
aritra	eretmos		oar.

From these and other words, too numerous to quote here, it may be safely inferred that the Aryans had already arrived at a state of society that settled itself in a city with a raja, tribal chief, but not a king, with padatis, footmen to guard the city and the agriculturists, carpenters, weavers, black-smiths, gold-smiths and others to work upon iron, silver and other metals. There is reason to believe that like the Greeks and the Romans who had no monarchical institution when they settled in Europe after leaving their original home, the Aryans of India had no monarchical organisation when they immigrated into India. The word Rajan which corresponds with Roman rex, chief, seems to have originally signified a chief or noble, but not a hereditary monarch. There are a few passages in the Vedas in which Rajan means merely a chief or a noble which in a number of other passages is used in the sense of a hereditary monarch. This variation in its sense is evidently due to the evolution of kingship from an original tribal chieftainship. Western scholars are inclined to believe that the normal, though not universal form of Government in early India was that by kings, as might be expected in view of the fact that Aryan Indians were invaders in a hostile territory: a situation which, as in the case of the Aryan invaders of Greece and of the German invaders of England, resulted almost necessarily in strengthening the monarchical element of the constitution.[6] 'It is also believed that the Vedic monarchy was sometimes hereditary and in others elective, though it is doubtful whether the election by the people was between the members of the royal family only or extended to members of all the noble clans.'[7] But sovereign power, if monarchical, must be either hereditary or for life of the person elected as a monarch. Such does not seem to be the case with sovereign power in the early Vedic period. As will be seen later on, persons elected to it were frequently expelled and restored. Frequent attempts to perform sacrificial offerings and spells for the attainment of sovereign power by different persons indicate that sovereign power in the early Vedic period was certainly democratic and insecure, based as it was on the ever-changing popular will, as shown by the frequent attempts of elected chiefs to control the popular passion by spells and witchcraft. The anarchical disturbance due to the frequent election, expulsion and restoration of chiefs seems to have led the people to establish monarchical form

---

[6] Vedic Index, Vol. II, p. 210.

[7] Vedic Index, Vol. II, p. 211.

of government on a hereditary basis, as stated both in the Kautiliya Arthasastra and the Mahabharata.[8] It is on the supposition of the evolution of hereditary monarchy out of an original democratic or tribal chieftainship that the use of the word Rajan both in the sense of a democratic leader and a hereditary king can find a satisfactory explanation. The following are the passages in which the word Rajan is used in the sense of a noble :—

" He amplifies his lordly might, with nobles (rajans) he slays, even mid alarms he dwells secure.

In great or lesser fight none checks him, none subdues,—the wielder of the thunderbolt." Rig., I. 40, 8.

Here the word rajabhih in plural means many kings, if it be taken in that sense. There cannot possibly be no more than a king to fight under the leadership of Indra.

" If in your dwelling, or at a noble's, or at a Brahman's, ye, Indra and Agni, holy ones, rejoice you,

Even from thence, ye mighty lords, come hither and drink libations of the flowing Soma." Rig., I. 108, 7.

As Indra and Agni are invoked to come and drink the libation of Soma in the sacrifice performed by a king, they cannot be thought of as lingering in another king's dwelling.

" O much invoked, may we subdue all famine and evil want with store of grain and cattle.

May we allied, as first in rank, with nobles obtain possessions by our own exertion." Rig., X. 42, 10.

There cannot be many kings with whom the priests can possibly ally themselves.

" He who hath store of herbs at hand like nobles amid an assembly of men,—physician is that sage's name, fiend-slayer, chaser of disease." Rig., X. 97, 6.

---

[8] Arthasastra, p. 16. (English translation). Mahabharata, Santi., Chap. 66.

There cannot possibly be many kings attending an assembly of people. Hence the word Rajanah must mean nobles here.

"Seize, Agni, on thy power and firmly hold it: Contend thou with the friend by way of friendship. Placed in the centre of our fellow nobles, Agni flash forth, frequently invoked here." A. V., II. 6, 4.

There cannt be many fellow kings. The word Sajata, fellow or born together, is an epithet qualifying the word "Rajnah," nobles.

"Make me beloved among the gods, beloved among the nobles, make me dear to every one who sees and to Sudra and to Aryan man." A. V., XIX. 62, 1.

There cannot be many kings in his place to whom the singer wants to endear himself.

"Bestow splendour on our Brahmans; bestow splendour on our nobles; bestow splendour on our Vaisyas and Sudras; bestow splendour over splendour on me."[9]

Here the sense of the word Rajasu can possibly be no other than nobles.

"Just as I speak in endearing terms to people, to Brahmans, nobles, Sudras, Aryans and even to my deadly foe, so may I become dear to gods, to the bestower of gifts; may my desire be fulfilled and I may realise this."[10]

Here like the words Brahmana, Sudra and Arya, the Rajanya means a class but not an individual. Hence it must mean nobles as a class. (Krishna Yajurveda, I. 3, 6) Since there is reason to believe that individual ownership of land in severalty was an established custom of Vedic India, it follows that frequent attempt at sacrificial

---

9 Tait. S., V. 7, 6, 4. Vaj. S., 18, 48.

10 Tait. S., I. 3, 6. Vaj. S., 26, 2.

performance for the possession of a village (grama) and of a kingdom (rashtra) must necessarily be rather for its overlordship than for the possession of the land. The Krishnayajurveda refers to ownership of land in severalty as follows :—

" He should make an offering to Indra and Agni on eleven potsherds who has a dispute about a field or with his neighbours." II. 2, 2.

The following sacrifices are enjoined for the attainment of lordship over a village or a kingdom :—

" He who desires a village should offer to the All-gods the sacrifice for taking possession. His equals are connected with All-gods ; verily he has recourse to the All-gods with their own share ; verily they subject his equals to him ; he becomes possessed of a village."[11] (Krishna Yajus, II. 3, 10.)

" They should be offered for one who desires the kingdom ; the Rashtrabhrits are the kingdom ; verily with the kingdom ; he wins the kingdom for him ; he becomes the kingdom ; they should be offeredfor oneself ; the Rashtrabhrits are the kingdom ; the people are the kingdom, cattle are the kingdom ; in that he becomes the highest, he is the kingdom. Verily with the kingdom he wins the kingdom, he becomes *the richest of his equals.* They should be offered for one who desires a village ; the Rashtrabhrits are the kingdom, *his fellows are the kingdom* ; he becomes possessed of a village. He offers on the dicing place ; verily on the dicing place *he wins his fellows for* him ; *being won they wait upon him.* They should be offered on the mouth of the chariot for him who desires force ; the Rashtrabhrits are the force ; verily by force he wins force for him ; he becomes possessed of force. They should be

---

[11] Compare Krishna Yaj., II. 2, 1. See also Appendix I.

offered for him who is expelled from his kingdom. To all his chariots he should say 'Be yoked'; verily he yokes the kingdom for him. The oblations of him whose realm is not in order are disordered. He should take off the right wheel of his chariot and offer in the box. So he puts in order his oblation; and the kingdom comes in order in accord with their coming into order." (Krishna Yaj., III. 4, 8.)

It is probable that recourse was had to dice-play and chariot-race to decide the claims of rival competitors for sovereign power over a village or kingdom. The statement that "on the dicing-place he wins his fellows and being won they wait upon him" found in above quotation confirms this view. The Lâtyâyana Srauta Sutra (VIII. 11, 1) also prescribes the Vajapeya for whomsoever the Brahmans and the Rajans may place at their head. Both in the Vajapeya and the Rajasuya dice-play and chariot-race form an important part of the rite. In the Rajasuya sacrifice the king (to be elected) is made to step on a tiger skin, under which is placed a piece of lead representing the head of Namuchi, on which he tramples. He then performs a chariot-race with sixteen other chariots and plays or deputes his Akshavapa, dice-player, to play at dice for him. It appears that his election to the sovereign power over the kingdom depended on his success in the chariot-race or in the dice-play or in both. In addition to war as a means to decide the claims of contending parties for power or possession, wrestling combat, chariot-race, or dice-play between two representatives of the contending parties seems to have been looked upon of old as a peaceful means to settle the question at issue. The rule seems to have been the underlying factor of the dice-play which is said to have been undertaken by ancient kings such as Nala and his brother Jayatsena or Pushkara and

Yudhishthira and Duryodhana,[12] in the very presence of their electors, the people and the priests.

There is also evidence to believe that perhaps owing to difficulties in deciding the claims of rival claimants to sovereign power or other causes, some states continued to successfully manage their affairs even without a king. Zimmer is said to have found in some Vedic passages states having no kings. This is stated in the Vedic Index of Macdonell and Keith :—

"Zimmer sees traces in one passsage of the Rigveda that in times of peace there was no king in some states the members of the royal family holding equal rights. He compares this with the state of affairs in early Germany. But the passage merely shows that the nobles could be called Rajan and is not decisive for the sense ascribed to it by Zimmer. Of course this state of affairs is perfectly possible and is exemplified later in Buddhistic times."[13]

The Rigveda passage referred to by him runs as follows :—

"Where a Brahman meets with herbs like nobles in an assembly, he is called a physician fiend-slayer and chaser of disease." X. 97, 6.

The Atharva Vedic passages which are believed by Zimmer to convey the same idea are I. 9; III. 4; and IV. 22.

1. "May Indra, Pushan, Varuna, Mitra, Agni benignant gods, maintain this man in riches.

May the Adityas and the Visvadevas set and support this man in supremest lustre.

---

[12] Arthasastra, V. III, 3.

[13] Vedic Index, Vol. II, p. 216.

2. May light, O gods, be around him, Agni, the sun, all that is bright and golden.

Prostrate beneath our feet his foes and rivals.
Uplift him to the loftiest cope off heaven.

3. Through that most mighty prayer, O Jatavedas, wherewith thou brought milk to strengthen Indra,

Even therewith exalt this man, O Agni, and give him highest rank among his fellows.

4. I have assumed this sacrifice, O Agni, their hopes,
Their glory and their riches' fulness.
Prostrate beneath our feet his foes and rivals
Uplift him to the loftiest cope of heaven."

A. V., I. 9.

This is clearly a sacrificial hymn or prayer to strengthen the claim of a candidate to sovereign power, whether strong or weak. It follows therefore that the state, to the lordship of which the candidate aspired, was in the meantime in a state of interregnum.

"To thee hath come the kingship with its splendour
On! shine as lord, sole ruler of the people.
King! let all regions of the heavens invite thee.
Here let men wait on thee and before thee. 1.

The tribesmen shall elect thee for the kingship,
These five celestial regions shall elect thee.
Rest on the height and top of kingly power; thence as a
Mighty man award us treasures 2.

Kinsmen, inviting thee, shall go to meet thee,
With thee go Agni as an active herald.
Let women and their sons be friendly minded.
Thou, mighty one, shalt see abundant tribute. 3.

First shall the Asvins, Varuna, and Mitra, the
Universal gods, and Maruts call thee.
Then turn thy mind to giving gifts of treasure,
Thence, mighty one, distribute wealth among us. 4.

Speed to us hither from the farthest distance
Propitious unto thee be Earth and Heaven.
Even so hath Varuna, this King, asserted, he who
Himself hath called thee: come thou hither. 5.

Pass to the tribes of men, O Indra, Indra.
Thou with the Varuna hast been found accordant.
To his own place this one (Agni) hath called thee, saying
'Let him adore the gods and guide the Clansmen.' 6.

The bounteous paths in sundry forms and places,
All in accord, have given thee room and comfort.
Let all these in concert call thee hither.
Live thy tenth decade here, a strong kind ruler." 7.

A. V., III. 4.

"Exalt and strengthen this my prince, O Indra,
Make him sole lord and leader of the people.
Scatter his foes, deliver all his rivals into his hand
In struggles for precedence. 1.

Give him a share in village, kine, and horses
And leave his enemy without a portion.
Let him as king be head and chief ot princes.
Give up to him, O Indra, every foeman. 2.

Let him be treasure-lord of goodly treasures,
Let him as king be master of the people.
Grant unto him great power and might, O Indra,
And strip his enemy of strength and vigour. 3.

Like milk kine yielding milk for warm libations,
Shower, Heaven and Earth, on him full many a blessing.

May he as king be Indra's well-beloved,
The darling of the kine, the plants, and the cattle. 4.

I join in league with thee Victorious Indra,
With whom men conquer and are never defeated.
He shall make thee the folk's sole lord and leader
Shall make thee highest of all human rulers. 5.

Supreme art thou, beneath thee are thy rivals,
And all, O king, who were thine adversaries.
Sole lord and leader and allied with Indra, bring,
Conquer, thy foemen's goods and treasures. 6.

Consume, with lion aspect, all their hamlets, with
Tiger aspect, drive away thy foemen.
Sole Lord and leader and allied, with Indra,
Seize, conquer, thine enemies' possessions." 7.

In the first of these two hymns, the elected king seems to have been an outsider, as he was expected to "speed thither from farthest distance." In the second, the right of the elected king to a share in the village-produce, and kine and horses in accordance with the custom of the monarchical states of those times is already clearly specified. It follows therefore that in these two instances the states were of a republican pattern in government.

Still more conclusive is the evidence furnished by the Aitareya and Taittiriya Brahmanas about the existence of republics during the Vedic period :—

"The Devas said, it is on account of our having no king that the Asuras defeat us. Let us elect a king. All consented. They elected Soma their king. Headed by King Soma, they were victorious in all directions." (Ait. Br., I. 14).

"The Devas and Asuras joined in battle. Then Prajapati concealed his eldest son Indra, lest he might be killed by the mighty Asuras. Prahlada, the son of Kayadhu likewise concealed his son Virochana, lest he might be killed by the Devas. The Devas went to Prajapati and said : there can possibly be no battle for a state having no king (for its leader). They courted Indra to be their king with sacrifices." (Tait. Br., I. 5, 9).

The Ambattha Suttanta of the Buddhists (I. 113) and the Arthasastra of Kautilya (XI. 1) refer in unmistakable terms to the existence of republics or corporations of warriors (Kshatriya Sreni) with the title of Rajans even so late as the Buddhistic period, when a greater portion of India was divided into a number of hereditary monarchical states.

Likewise both the Arthasastra (I. 13) and the Mahabharata (Rajadharma Parva, Chapter 67) speak of a period when the Aryans had no monarchical institutions, and elected Manu to be their king for the first time in their history.

Hence it may be safely asserted that when the Aryans invaded India, they were divided into a number of Gaṇas or Janas corresponding to the Roman Gens and Gentes and the Greek Genos, each Gens being a republic or democracy with no king, and that during the Vedic and Brahminic periods a number of the Janas passed into elective monarchies, while a few retained their republican form even so late as the Buddhist period.[14]

We have no reliable information as to what their economical and administrative condition was at the remote period. Still from what Hindu astrologers traditionally say of planetary constitution with reference to its influence on the economic and administrative condition of human society, some information may be gathered about the

[14] Buddhist India by Rhys Davids, p. 19.

economical and administrative constitution of the republics. According to the astrologers the planetary world is believed to consist of nine primary Nayakas or lords, such as a king, minister, commander of the army, superintendent of crops, superintendent of grains, superintendent of barter (argha), superintendent of clouds, superintendent of liquids, and that of dry things. Then there are seven secondary leaders, as the lords of horses, of elephants, of cows, of sheep, of buffaloes, of camels, and of asses. Then a set of ten subordinate lords, such as lords of gods, of men, of wealth, of cloth, of gems, of women, of trees, of beasts, of goods, and of trade. Then follows a set of five, as lords of the treasury, of war, of ornaments, of edict (ajna) and of transactions. Then another set of five, as the lords of learning, of happiness, of counsel, of work, and of bravery. The division of these 36 lords into five groups is evidently an indication of successive later additions. Accordingly they may be reduced to nine, as (1) a lord of war, (2) a lord of crops, (3) one of grains, (4) one of trade and barter, (5) one of cattle and beasts, (6) one of water, (7) one of forests, (8) one of clothings and implements and (9) one of disputes (Vyavahara).

Of these, the duty of the lord of war is clear enough and it is he on whom lay the most important duty, the protection of the gens against enemies. The duty of the one of the two lords of crops and grains seems to have been the supervision of crops and harvests and protection of them from wild tribes and beasts. In the absence of currency it was not an easy task to settle the rate of barter of things and a separate officer seems to have been appointed for the purpose of fixing the rate, at which things had to be bartered. The lord of cattle had to lead the cattle of the gens as a whole to pasture and graze them and bring them back to the village in the evening, as is still a custom in a number of villages even now. The duty of the lord of water was evidently the regulation of water of the village tank or lake, or river for drinking or irrigation of crops. The appointment of a lord of clothings and implements was of course for the purpose of giving facilities for the production of clothing and weaving and agricultural implements. Lastly it was the duty of the lord of disputes, to settle the civil disputes of the people and to punish the criminals, perhaps following the opinion of the village elders assembled in the public ground or hall on important cases. If there was a lord of learning in addition, he might have been the village priest whose business was, as still prevalent in a number of villages, to perform the sacrifices, to conduct the marriages, funerals and religious functions, to fix the time of sowing and reaping and to impart knowledge to the village boys. It need not be stated that all these officers were maintained, as they are even now, at the expense of the village as a whole.

Land was held in severalty[15] and each family devoted itself to its agricultural or industrial pursuits severally. Hunting, fishing, collection of forest produce, repair of village tanks and other big projects were, as they are even now, carried out on communal or co-operative basis. Lending and borrowing of grains at interest was a prevalent custom. Division of parental property among the male children during or after the life of the father was an established custom even during the Vedic period.[16] Caste was unknown, but the people were divided into four classes, the Brahmans, Kshatriyas, Vaisyas, and the Sudras. There was intermarriage among the classes, the lower class,

[15] Tait. Samhita, II. 3, 1.

[16] Tait Samhita, II. 6.1. See also Appendix II.

however, not being permitted to marry a maiden of an upper class. There was interdining among the four classes, the Sudras being employed as cooks. Gambling was a painful vice of the times. Even kings lost their kingdoms and even their wives by taking to gambling.

Such seems to be in brief the nature of the little republics of the Indian Aryans when they invaded and occupied the North Western parts of India. Whether this deserves the name of a republic or democracy or tribal state of society is a question that may be conveniently left to the taste of historians.

LECTURE II

ELECTIVE MONARCHY

The division of the Hindus originally into four classes, the Brahmans, the Kshatriyas, the Vaisyas, and the Sudras and later into rigid castes bearing the same names is of Indian origin, as no trace of such division is found among the Greeks, the Romans, and other branches of the Indo-European race. It is true that the Aryans of the West, too, had their priests, warriors, traders, and husbandmen like their brethren of India, but still there was not among them such distinct classification of social grades which, with later restrictions as to *connubium* and *commensality*, easily passed into isolated castes. Nor are the class names Indo-European in origin. Even in some election hymns, the elected man is found designated not even as a Kshatriya, but merely as man by the use of the demonstrative pronoun 'this.' It is probable therefore that the word Kshatriya, protector from wounds, is a later Indian or Indo-Iranian word derived to designate a separate class of later formation. So long as no need was felt for the institution of a separate Kshatriya class to defend the hearth and home of the invading Aryans, the general term used to designate a king elected for life or for a definite period was Raja, noble, corresponding to the Roman *Rex*. It is a historical fact admitted by almost all Western scholars that when the Aryans invaded India, their leaders were not monarchs, but brave warriors elected for the occasion.[17] Such occasional election of a warrior to defend them against their external enemies, does not seem to have answered their purpose after they settled themselves in the country. They

---

[17] Rig., X. 173. A.V., I. 9; Tait. Samhita, I. 8, 10.

seem to have felt the need for the election of a permanent chief to be at their head and carry on the internal administration of their settlements. This view is corroborated both by the Arthasastra and the Mahabharata. The Arthasastra says (I. 13) :—

" People, suffering from anarchy as illustrated by the proverbial tendency of a large fish swallowing a small one, first elected Manu Vaivasvata to be their king and allotted one-sixth of the grains grown and one-tenth of the merchandise as sovereign dues."[18]

How they elected their king, and whom they elected and for what period are questions that cannot be satisfactorily answered. It is probable that as dice-play and chariot race are found forming part of the coronation rite, the successful candidate in one or two of those games seems to be the one that was selected by the people for the coveted post.[19] The statement made in the Rigveda (X. 34, 8) that the king himself pays homage and reveres the dice does not seem to mean a gamester's respect to an amusement. Though at a later period when hereditary monarchy was firmly established in the land, these two games in connection with the coronation rite of the kings had become merely symbolic, there is no reason to disbelieve that their connection with the rite originated from the custom of making the kingdom a reward for success in the games. Though the proffered prize in a chariot race was a thousand cattle (Rig., VI. 45), there is no reason to believe that the prize in all cases was of the same kind, but never a kingdom.[20]

The trouble which an elected chief had to contend against seems to have been threefold : trouble due to

---

[18] Vedic Index, Vol. II, p. 20. Mahabharata, Rajadharma Parva, Chap. 67.

[19] Tai. Samhita, I. 8, 10-11 and II. 2, 1.

[20] Rig., VIII. 70 and II. 31.

external foes or aboriginal people, and that due to his own kinsmen, and lastly his disagreement with the assembly of the people. In the earliest period when a separate Kshatriya class was not yet established, the only trouble which the elected chief or Raja had to contend against was the frequent attack of the Aryan settlements by the aboriginal people. In the course of time the Aryans seem to have got rid of this partly by conquering and enslaving the native tribes and partly by taking them into the Aryan fold by extending to them right of connubium and commensality. The employment of Sudras as cooks and servants in the houses of even the Aryan priests, the marriage[21] of Sudra women by the Aryans, and the privilege,[22] granted to the sons of Brahmans by Sudra wives, of becoming Brahmans and of exercising even priestly functions are historical instances of the conciliatory policy of the invaders. Even enslaved men and women of the Sudras seem to have been allowed to take part in the most solemn sacrifices of the Aryans. Milking the cows in sacrifices is a function entrusted to Sudras and the completion of the Gavam Ayana sacrifice is marked by the dancing of Sudra women. That at a later period of the history of the Aryans Sudras were allowed even the right of becoming kings in many of the Aryan kingdoms, is an undeniable historical fact. Why the Chandalas were not granted rights and privileges similar to those which the Sudras succeeded in getting from the Aryans, is a question that requires further investigation. It is however probable that they belonged to an earlier aboriginal race, too firmly inclined to its own wild and loathsome way of living.

[21] Kalivarjya prakarana, Smritichandrika, Vol. I.

[22] Lâtyâyana Srautasutra, Dasapeya Sacrifice.

When the troubles due to aboriginal race were thus removed, the priestly class together with the people seem to have turned their attention to the question of electing a king. It was a question of internal administration. A skilful administrator, capable of governing the people in accordance with their customs, and with no domestic troubles of his own, was the one that was urgently needed. The priests seem to have thought that a bachelor king with no domestic ties of his own would best serve their purpose. Accordingly they seem to have established an institution of queens, on the eldest of whom it was, as will be shown later on, the duty of the chief priest to beget a prince. It appears that the prince had to live a celebate life and rule the kingdom in accordance with the wishes of the people's assembly. While this new departure removed the inherent difficulties of election, it seems to have occasioned some new troubles. There seems to have arisen a new class of princes or Kshatriyas, as they were called, and while the kinsmen of the ruling prince endeavoured to snatch the kingdom in the interests of some one else of their own class, the ruling princes themselves, one after another, seem to have been fighting with the priests for their own right of marriage and for hereditary monarchy. In some Aryan settlements the priests seem to have made a compromise with their rulers and set up hereditary monarchies while in others, the dispute between the priests and the rulers seems to have occasioned a civil war which, as will be seen later on, ended disastrously for the priests. These and other troubles of elective monarchy are clearly hinted, if not expressed, in the following election hymns of the Rigveda and Atharvaveda :—

"And they (the Asuras), like people who elect their rulers, have in abhorrence turned away from Vritra."[23]

[23] Rig., X. 124, 8.

1. "Be with us; I have chosen thee: stand steadfast and immoveable.

Let all the people wish for thee; let not thy kingship fall away.

2. Be even here; fall not away: be like a mountain unremoved.

Stand steadfast here like Indra's self, and hold the kingship in thy grasp.

3. This man hath Indra established, made secure by strong oblations' power.

May Soma speak a benison, and Brahmanaspati on him.

4. Firm is the sky and firm the earth, steadfast also are the hills.

Steadfast is all this living world, and steadfast is this king of men.

6. On constant Soma let us think with constant sacrificial gift.

And then may Indra make the *class bring tribute* unto thee alone." Rig., X. 173.

2. "Subduing those who rival us, subduing all malignities.

Withstand the man who menaces, withstand the man who angers us.

3. Soma and Savitar, the gods, have made thee a victorious king.

All elements have aided thee, to make thee general conqueror.

5. Slayer of rivals, rivalless, victorious, with royal sway, over these beings may I rule.

May I be sovereign of the folk."[24]

The points to be noticed in these three hymns are (1) right of the people to elect, (2) the custom of collecting

---

[24] Rigveda, X. 174. Compare A. V., VI. 87.

tribute or tax from the clans or people as contrasted from priests who were exempt from taxation, (3) and the trouble due to rivals.

"The Being lays the sap of life in beings : he hath become the sovereign lord of creatures.

Yama comes to this man's royal consecration : let him as king own and allow this kingdom.

2. Come forward, turn not back in scorn, strong guardian, slayer *of thy foes.*

Approach, O Gladdener of thy friends, the Gods have blessed and strengthened thee.

3. All waited on him as he came to meet them. He self-resplendent moves endued with glory.

That is the royal hero's lofty nature! he, manifold, hath gained immortal powers.

4. Stride forth to heaven's broad regions, thou, a tiger, on a tiger's skin.

Let all the *people* long for thee; let heavenly floods be rich in milk.

5. Heaven's waters joyous in their milk, the waters of the middle air and those that earth containeth—

I with the gathered power and might of all these waters sprinkle thee.

6. The heavenly waters rich in milk have sprinkled thee with power and might to be the Gladdener of thy friends. May Savitar so fashion thee.

These, compassing the tiger, rouse the lion to great joy and bliss.

As strong floods purify the standing ocean,
So men adorn the leopard in the waters."

A. V., IV. 8.

"1. I win the love of Indra that his friend may reach yet higher state.

Increase, as rain the grass, *this man's dominion* and his lofty fame.

2. *Confirm the princely* power in him, Agni and Soma grant him wealth.

In all the circuit of his rule make him yet higher for your friend.[25]

3. *The man who shows us enmity*, whether *a stranger* or akin,

Thou wilt give up entire to me who sacrifice and press the juice." (A. V., VI. 54.)

Observe the keen anxiety felt here for the security of the kingly power, due to enemies both internal and external.

" 1. Firm is the sky, firm the earth, and firm is all this living world.

Firm are the mountains on their base and stedfast is this king of men.

2. Stedfast may Varuna the king, stedfast the god Brihaspati,

Stedfast may Indra, stedfast, too, may Agni keep thy stedfast reign.

3. Firm, never to be shaken, crush thy foemen, under thy feet lay those who strive against thee.

One-minded, true to thee be all the regions; faithful to thee, the firm, be this assembly." (A. V., VI. 88.)[26]

The important point worthy of notice in the above hymn is the dependence of the kingly power on the faithfulness of the assembly.—

" 1. Do ye, O Brahmanaspati, invest for royal sway this man

With that wherewith the deities invested Savitar the god.

---

[25] Compare A. V., I. 9; and IV. 22.

[26] Compare A. V., VI. 86.

2. Invest this Indra for long life, invest him for great princely power,

That I may lead him on to eld, that he may watch his princedom long.

3. Invest this Soma for long life, invest him for great hearing power,

That I may lead him on to eld, that he may watch over hearing long.

4. For us, surround him, cover him with splendour,

Give him long life and death when age removes him.

This garment hath Brihaspati presented to Soma, to the king, to wrap about him.

5. Advance to good old age! endue the mantle. Be thou *our heifers' guard from imprecation* (Grishtinam abhisastipa).

Live thou a hundred full and plenteous autumns and wrap thee in prosperity of riches.

6. Thou for our weal hast clothed thee in this garment, thou hast become our *cow's sure guard from curses* (Vasanam abhisastipa).

Live thou a hundred full and plenteous autumns: thou living, fair thyself, shalt deal forth treasures.

7. In every need, in every fray we call, as friends to succour us, Indra the mightiest of all.

Gold coloured, undecaying, surrounded with heroes, dwell, dying in old age, with people round thee.

8. This is the spoken word of Agni, Soma, Brihaspati, and Savitar, and Indra." (A. V., XIX. 34.)

"Desiring bliss, at first, light-finding Rishis began religious rite and holy fervour.

Thence energy was born, and might, and kingship;

So this man let gathered gods incline them."

A. V., XIX. 41.

While hymn No. 41 gives to the Rishis the credit of establishing elective monarchy, the other hymn (No. 24) seems to restrict the period of monarchy to the life of the elected individual, as clearly pointed out in verses 6 and 7. The people's call on the elected king to be their heifers' guard and the assumed consent of the king to be their cows' sure guard from curses is evidently a reference to the occasional condemnation of the institution of queens or cows on the part of a few elected kings. The motive for hurling imprecations on cows can have no satisfactory explanation unless cows are taken to mean queens, the mothers of the Kshatriyas. This question will, however, be discussed at length in connection with the origin of Kshatriyas later on. What is however meant by the imprecations and curses of the cows is the attempt of the bachelor kings to put an end to the institution of queens on whom the Brahmans had the right of begetting the ruling princes and the warrior Kshatriyas, and to establish hereditary monarchy in its stead by marrying themselves. So long as the Kshatriyas could not succeed in their attempt to set up hereditary monarchies, the ruling kings, though bachelors, were not free from troubles. While they had to contend on the one hand with their brother princes who seem to have made frequent attempts to evict the elected king and seize the throne, the trouble due to the dissatisfaction of the people on the other seems to have been also immense. This two-fold trouble is referred to in the following hymns of the Atharvaveda :—

" 1. This parna-amulet hath come, strong and destroying with its strength my rivals.

The power of the gods, the plants' sweet essence,

May it incite me ceaselessly with vigour.

2. O Parna-amulet, in me set firmly might and opulence.

Within the compass of my rule may I be rooted and supreme.

That dear mysterious amulet which gods have set within the tree.

3. May the gods grant to me to wear together with extended life.

As gift, by Varuna instructed, Parna hath come, the mighty strength of Soma.

4. This would I, brightly shining, love and cherish for long life lasting through a hundred autumns.

5. The Parna-charm hath come to me for great security from ill.

That I may be exalted, yea, above the wealth of Aryaman.

6. Sagacious builders of the car, clever and skilful artisans,—

Make all the men on every side, Parna, obedient to my will.

7. *The nobles and makers of the kings, troopleaders, masters of the horse,*

Make all the men on every side, Parna, obedient to my will.

Thou, Parna, art my body's guard, man kin by birth to me a man.

With splendour of the circling year, I bind thee, on me, Amulet!" (A. V., III. 5.)

"We bend together all your (kinsmen's) minds, your vows and purposes we bend.

We bend together you who stand apart with hopes opposed to ours.

I with my spirit seize and hold your spirits.

Follow with thought and wish my thoughts and wishes.

I make your hearts the thralls of my dominion!

On me attendant come the way I guide you."

A. V., III. 8, 5-6.

"Unanimous, ye kinsmen, come united, come to the glory of this mighty guardian.

The inclination which your hearts have harboured, the purpose which hath occupied your spirits,

This I annul with sacrifice and butter.

In me be your sweet resting place, O Kinsmen.

Stand even here, forsake me not. Before us may

Pushan make your path unfit to travel."

A. V., VI. 73, 1-3.

"Close gathered be your bodies! be your minds and vows in unison!

Here present Brahmanaspati and Bhaga have assembled you.

Let there be union of your minds, let there be union of your hearts.

Ah that is troubled in your lot with this I mend and harmonize.

As, free from jealousy, the strong Adityas have been the Vasu's and Rudra's fellows,

So free from jealousy, Lord of three titles!

Cause thou *these people* here to be one-minded."

A. V., VI. 74.

"We bend your minds in unison, bend in harmony your hopes and plans.

You, there, who turn to sundered ways, we bend and bow in unison.

I with my spirit make your spirits captive!

These with their thoughts follow my thoughts and wishes.

I make your hearts submissive to mine orders;

Closely attending go where I precede you."

A. V., VI. 94.

"Subdue with conquering might his other *rivals, those yet unborn* repel, O Jatavedas.

For great felicity protect this kingdom, and in this man let all the gods be joyful."

A. V., VII. 35.

"To me hath this word given by Agni, fame, force and might, and strength and life and lustre.

May Agni, too, bestow on me three times a hundred manly powers.

For mighty strength, for action, I receive thee, for manly power, to last a hundred autumns.

For conquering strength, and energy and vigour.

I fasten thee, for chieftainship, for bearing royal *dominion through a hundred autumns*."[27]

A. V., XIX. 37.

While it is clearly stated in these and other hymns that the troubles of the elected monarch were due to chariot-makers, artisans, troopleaders, masters of the horse, the king-makers or priests, his kinsmen, and lastly the people at large, there is no mention made in any of the hymns of troubles due to sons and wives, a lurking domestic danger, prevalent at a later period, as set forth in the Arthasastra of Kautilya.[28]

The custom mentioned in A. V., XIX. 37 of fastening an amulet with the desire of making the kingship last through a hundred years points to the election of individuals to kingship only for life. This is confirmed also by the steps taken by the people to dethrone and banish an elected chief on account of his oppression and misgovernment. The banishment of an elected chief

---

[27] *Cf.* A. V., VI. 97; VII. 78; 96.

[28] Artha., Book I. Chaps. 17, 18, 20, 21.

and the restoration of an expelled king are thus alluded to in the following hymns of the Atharvaveda :—

" This thunderbolt shall take its fill of order,
Scare life away and overthrow the kingdom,
Tear necks in pieces, rend the hopes asunder,
Even as the lord of might the neck of Vritra.

Down, down beneath the conqueror, let him not rise, concealed in earth, but lie down-smitten, with the bolt.

Seek out the fierce oppressor, yea, strike only the oppressor dead.

Down on the fierce oppressor's head strike at full length, O thunderbolt." (A. V., VI. 134.)

1. Loudly he roared. Here let him labour deftly. Spread, Agni, over spacious earth and heaven.

Let Maruts who possess all treasures yoke thee. Bring him who reverently paid oblations.

2. Though he be far away, let the red horses bring,
Indra, bring the sage to us and friendship,
Since with Sautramani the gods for him overpower
Gayatri, Brihati, and hymn of praises.

3. King Varuna call thee hither from the waters !
From hill, and mountains Soma call thee hither !
Let Indra call thee hither to these people.
Fly hither to these people as a falcon.

4. May the hawk bring the man who must be summoned.
From far away, *in alien land, an exile.*
May both the Asvins make thy path-way easy.
Come and unite yourself with him, ye kinsmen.

5. Let thine opponents call thee back.
Thy friends have chosen thee again.
Indra and Agni, all the gods have kept thy home amid the tribe.

He who disputes our calling thee, be he a stranger or akin,

Drive him, O Indra, far away, and do thou bring this man to us."[29] (A. V., III. 3.)

The Taittiriya Samhita also enjoins a sacrifice[30] for the purpose of averting an impending expulsion of a king as follows :—

"'O Aditi, do thou confirm'; with these words he who is being expelled should take the foot-dust of him (who is expelling). 'Aditi is this earth. Verily she confirms the kingdom for him.'" (II. 3. 1.)

The peaceful and quiet performances of necessary sacrifices in accordance with the belief of those times to celebrate the grand events of the election of a new king or of the restoration of an exiled king clearly indicates that it was no revolutionary act attended with bloodshed. Nor is there any reason to suppose that kingship during the Vedic period, whether elective or hereditary, was quite insecure and that no king's life was safe. Considering the frequent election of kings to vacancies caused by death or expulsion of elected chiefs on account of their unfitness, the election and restoration hymns that are still preserved in the Vedas appear to be too few. To interpret them as a sure sign of the insecurity of royal power is to forget the necessity which the invading Aryans had for showing their united front against the hostile aboriginal tribes. The spells, charms, and sacrifices, performed by chiefs to recover their lost sovereignty or the loyal affection of their kinsmen or of the people at large point rather to the natural administrative difficulty of the times than to tyrannical designs of the royal clans or to the

---

[29] Compare A. V., I. 29 and III. 4.

[30] For having recourse to sacrifice as a political weapon, see Appendix I.

turbulent nature of the people. So long as the kings made no attempts to establish hereditary monarchies in the place of elective monarchy of the early period, they could rely on the strong support of the priests and the people against their clansmen. It is only at a later period of the history of the Aryans in India that we hear of a terrible internecine civil war between the Brahmans and the Kshatriyas, as illustrated by the conflict between Visvamitra and Vasishtha and Parasurama and the Kartaviryas. By that time the Aryans seem to have succeeded in so firmly establishing themselves in the land and in so skilfully and carefully solving the race-question by taking the aboriginal Sudras into the Aryan fold, extending to them the right of connubium and commensalism that there was no alien race-question at the time of the civil war to make the situation worse for the Aryans. It follows, therefore, that royal power was neither insecure nor elective sometimes and hereditary at others, as Macdonell and Keith are inclined to believe.[31]

It was quite secure and was quite powerful to show its united front to the hostile Dasyus or natives so as to Aryanise them partly by conquest and partly by conciliatory measures. It was also elective and of the same constitutional type that is still prevalent in the South Indian States of Travancore and Cochin, of which it is, as will be seen later on, the source. This elective monarchy continued till it was set aside by hereditary monarchy somewhere about the times of Visvamitra and Parasurama.[32]

---

[31] Vedic Index, Vol. II, p. 811.

[32] 1700 B. C. (See Gavam Ayana, the Vedic Era.)

LECTURE III

THE ORIGIN OF THE KSHATRIYAS

Before going to read my paper on the Origin of the Kshatriyas, I think it necessary to draw your attention to some of the important points noted in my paper on "The Evolution of Castes," which I read in the Mythic Society at Bangalore some years ago.

I. The most important point to which I want to draw your attention is the meaning of the word caste. Caste means a social exclusiveness with reference to diet and marriage. So long as a Hindu, whether a Brahman, Kshatriya, Vaisya or Sudra, observes his social or communal rules about the articles of diet he eats and about the woman he marries, he is regarded to maintain his caste and to lose it the moment he infringes the rules of dietary and marriage. Birth and rituals are secondary, for there is evidence to prove that the offspring of Brahmans and non-Brahman women used to become Brahmans and that religious rites were changed from time to time.

Even now all that people care to know about a man's observance of his caste is where he eats and what he eats and whom he has married. These two things are visible while birth and observance of rituals are invisible. The Lords and Commons of England, now two classes, will become two castes the moment they cease to intermarry and interdine with each other.

II. The next point to be noticed is that the Hindus of the pre-Buddhistic period had no such rules of diet and marriage as prevented them from interdining and intermarrying with other people. Animal food and liquor also formed part of their diet.[33]

They married women of other races also. Usually a Brahman had four wives corresponding to the four classes; Kshatriya, three; Vaisya, two; and a Sudra one or many of his own class. They all employed Sudra cooks in their houses. Sons begotten by Brahmans on non-Brahman women were free to exercise the functions of Brahmans.[34] Hence the words, Brahmans, Kshatriyas, Vaisyas and Sudras were names of classes rather than of castes during the pre-Buddhistic period.

III. With the appearance of Buddhism, all this changed. Though Buddhism did not preach caste, it vehemently denounced certain customs, the disappearance of which brought about caste into existence. It denounced flesh-eating and plurality of wives and denied Nirvana to those who were addicted to animal sacrifices, flesh-eating and sexual indulgence. The Brahmans gave up those two condemned customs and, as a result, formed themselves into castes mainly with the intention of keeping up their dietary and marriage rules. The other classes, too, followed them and formed separate castes.

This is the summary of my paper on the evolution of castes and as the second part of that paper has important bearing on the subject under consideration, I am going to read it before you once more.

If words have their own biography to tell, as Professor Max Muller once put it, there are some Vedic words and hymns that appear to tell a tale different from what later Puranic writers took them to mean. The words that appear to have played an important

---

[33] *Vide* Apastamba.

[34] *Vide* Lâtyâyana, IX. 2, 6 and Apastamba, II. 5, 11.

part in the history of the origin of the Kshatriya class are (1) Brahmajâya, (2) Brahmagavi, (3) Vaśa, (4) Prisni, (5) Go, and (6) Kâmadhenu. Of these the first five are Vedic and the last Puranic. The literal meaning of the first word 'Brahmajâya' is the wife of a Brahman or priest, and it is used in that sense both in the Rigveda (X. 109) and the Atharvaveda. (V. 17). Her abduction by a Kshatriya or rather a Kshatriya King and her subsequent restoration to her husband, the priest, form the subject matter of the two hymns in which that word occurs.

The word 'Brahmagavi' means the cow of a Brahman or priest and is used in that sense in the fifth hymn of the twelfth Kanda of the Atharvaveda.

The word 'Vasa,' a barren or powerful cow, as interpreted by Sayana and others, is found in the fourth hymn of the twelfth Kanda of the same Veda.

The word 'Go,' a Brahman's or priest's cow, is found in the eighteenth and nineteenth hymns of the fifth Kanda of the Atharvaveda. The disastrous consequences that would befall a Kshatriya or King, if he were to rob a priest of his cow, are elaborately described in these four hymns.

The word 'Prisni,' a wonderful cow, occurs in the eleventh hymn of the fifth Kanda of the Atharvaveda, and the subject matter of that hymn is a conversation between Varuna and an Atharvan priest about the possession of a wonderful cow bestowed by the former on the latter.

The story of a terrible war between Visvamitra, a Puranic King, who is said to have become a Brahman by the performance of a penance, and Vasishtha, a Vedic priest, on account of the latter's Kâmadhenu or desire-giving cow which Visvamitra is said to have attempted to take for himself by force is elaborately described in all the Puranas. Likewise the story of the destruction of King

Kartavirya and his family and also of other Kshatriyas by Parasurama to avenge the death of his father Jamadagni who was murdered by Kartavirya for the sake of the priest's cow is found in almost all the Puranas. Almost all oriental scholars have followed Sayana in taking the words, Brahmagavi, Vasa, Prisni, Go, and Kamadhenu to mean a cow of extraordinary powers in the possession of such famous Vedic priests as Vasishtha, Jamadagni, and others. But line 33 of the fourth hymn of the fifth Kanda of the Atharvaveda, where Vasa or a cow is said to be the mother of a Rajanya or King, seems to suggest that the so-called cow is not a quadruped beast but a woman, the same as Brahmajaya or a priest's wife whose abduction by Kshatriyas seems to have been the cause of a number of feuds between the Brahmans on the one hand and the Kshatriyas on the other. If reliance can be placed upon this plain interpretation of the word, Vasa, and if it can be extended to all the cow-hymns, then what has hitherto appeared to be an inexplicable myth resolves itself into a credible historical episode, evidencing an institution or custom, the like of which is still prevalent in what is called the land of Parasurama, *i.e.*, the States of Travancore and Cochin. The peculiar Vedic custom that can be based upon this interpretation and which has become extinct outside the States of Travancore and Cochin appears to have been somewhat as follows :—

There seems to have been an institution of women, called Brahmajayas, Brahmagavis, Vasas or Cows, whom the priests had the exclusive privilege to marry. The Kshatriya class seems to have been the result of the union of these women with the Brahman priests. The eldest son of the high priest and the chief Brahmajaya seems to have been invested with ruling powers while the sons of other priests and other Brahmajayas formed a band of soldiers or militia. Neither the king nor the soldiers seem to have been allowed to marry. The fifth verse of the Brahmajaya hymn where a bachelor is said to have restored to Brihaspati or the chief priest, his consort seems to suggest the above idea. The kings of several states seem to have protested against this custom and themselves married the Brahmajayas or Brahmagavis. This breach of custom on the part of the Kshatriyas apparently brought about the occasional feuds between the Brahmans and the Kshatriyas, as implied by the Brahmajaya and other hymns. The war between Visvamitra and Vasishta as well as that between Parasurama and Kartavirya seem to have been due to the same cause. Visvamitra seems to have fought for the right of Kshatriyas to marry and appears to have brought about the marriage of Rama, Lakshmana, Bharata, and Satrughna with the foster daughters of Janaka and his brother, as a protest against this custom. This violation of the custom on the part of Visvamitra seems to have provoked Parasurama and led him to wage war with Rama and his brothers on their way to Ayodhya after the marriage. It is probable that Parasurama, the champion of the Brahmans, failed in his attempt to subdue the Kshatriyas and to re-establish the privileged custom of the priestly class. It is also probable, though partly contrary to the Puranic version of the story, that being defeated and driven out by the victorious Kshatriyas, he came with a few followers to the west-coast of South India and set up a colony there, perpetuating the old custom, which is still prevalent in Travancore and Cochin and which is attributed to him. It appears that the ruling kings in these two states are princes begotten by a family or sect of Brahman priests on a successive line of princesses or queens like the Vedic Brahmajayas whose male issues were originally, though not now, obliged to live a celebate life with ruling powers, while the female issues became the queens of the state in succession. There is no marriage system among the Nayars, nor do the women confine themselves to a single husband. The Brahmans in these states are called Nambudris and they observe the Vedic customs. The following extracts, taken out from Thurston's *Castes and Tribes of Southern India* and Gopal Panikar's *Malabar and its Folk*, corroborate the above facts :—

"As recorded in the Keralamahatmya, tradition traces the Nambudris to Ahikshetra, whence Parasurama invited Brahmans to settle in his newly reclaimed territory. In view of preventing the invited settlers from relinquishing it he is said to have introduced, on the advice of the sage Narada, certain deep and distinctive changes in their personal, domestic, and communal institutions."[35]

"Writing in the eighteenth century, Hamilton observes that the Nambudris are the first in both capacities of Church and State, and some of them are Popes, being sovereign princes in both."[36]

"He is perhaps, as his measurements seem to prove, the truest Aryan in Southern India, and not only physically, but in his customs, habits and ceremonies which are so welded into him that forsake them he cannot, if he would."[37]

"Every Nambudri is, theoretically, a life-long student of the Vedas."[38]

"The eldest son alone marries. Should a Nambudri's eldest son die, the next marries and so on. Women join the family of their husband and to this too her children belong ....If there is no male member, the Sarvasvâdanam

[35] Castes and Tribes of Southern India, Vol. V, p. 154.

[36] *Ibid*, p. 156.

[37] *Ibid*, p. 157.

[38] *Ibid*, p. 160.

marriage is performed by which a man of another family is brought into the family and married to a daughter of it, who, after the manner of the "appointed daughter" of old Hindu Law, hands on the property through her children."[39]

"An exception to this general rule of inheritance is that seventeen families of Payanmur in North Malabar follow the Marumakkattayam system of inheritance through the female line. The other Nambudris look askance at these, and neither marry nor dine with them. It is supposed that they are not pure bred, having Kshatriya blood in their veins."[40]

"Hamilton, writing concerning Malabar at the end of the seventeenth and the beginning of the eighteenth century, says, that 'when the Zamorin marries, he must not cohabit with his bride till the Nambudri or chief priest has enjoyed her, and, if he pleases, may have three nights of her company, because the first fruit of her nuptials must be an holy oblation to the god he worships, and some of the nobles are so complaisant as to allow the clergy the same tribute, but the common people cannot have that compliment paid to them, but are forced to supply the priest's place themselves." [41]

"The Nambudris call themselves Arya Brahmanas. Their legendary transmigration to Malabar from Northern India is doubtless true. There is by far the purest form of the Vedic Brahmanism to be met with in Southern India. A complete account of the religion of the Nambudris cannot be given in these pages. The Nambudri's life is a round of sacrifices, the last of which is the burning of

[39] Castes and Tribes of Southern India, Vol. V, p. 176.

[40] *Ibid*, p. 177.

[41] *Ibid*, p. 176.

his body on the funeral pyre. When the Nambudri has no male issue, he performs the Putrakameshti or Karmavipâka Prâyaschittam Yâgams or sacrifices to obtain it."[42]

"According to the Brahman tradition, the Nayar caste is the result of union between the Nambudris with Deva, Gandharva, and Rakshasa women introduced by Parasurama; and this tradition embodies the undoubted fact that the caste by its practice of hypergamy has had very large infusion of Aryan blood."[43]

"The original Nayars were undoubtedly a military body, holding lands and serving as a militia, but the present Nayar caste includes persons who, by hereditary occupation, are traders, artisans, oil mongers palanquin bearers, and even barbers and washermen."[44]

"They (the Brahmans) are the lords of the soil, possessing large powers for oppression and domination over the labouring classes, the Nayars. All the domestic concerns of the Nayars, all their social intercourses, all their liberty of thought and action are regulated by the arbitrary will of the Brahman priests. Not one of them, in their true capacity, is allowed to move his little finger except on consultation with the Brahman priests; and disobedience to their orders is often visited with their displeasure and the resulting deprivation of their means of livelihood and banishment from society."[45]

"The Aryan Brahmans, when they came into the country, had the same social organisation as exists among their successors to-day. Their laws strictly ordain that only the eldest member of the household shall be left free to enter into lawful wedlock with a woman of their caste, the

[42] Castes and Tribes of Southern India, Vol. V, *Ibid*, p. 235.

[43] p. 211.

[44] *Ibid*, p. 284.

[45] *Ibid*, p. 284.

younger members being left to shift for themselves in this matter. In ancient times the only asylum which these latter could find in the existing state of their social circumstances was in the Nayar families which settled round about them. It should, in this connection, be remembered that the Brahmans formed an aristocratic order, and as such they were the exclusive custodians and expositors of the law. Naturally enough, too large numbers of Brahman younger sons who were looking about for wives, turned to the Nayar families and began to enter into illegitimate unions of the nature of concubinage. Now the sanctity of formal and religious marriages was incompatible with looseness and degradation involved in these illegitimate unions; and Brahman ingenuity discovered a ready means of getting over the difficulty by a social prohibition of valid marriages among the Nayars, which would otherwise have prejudicially interfered with their conjugal destinies."[46]

In order to show how far the Vedic hymns 'Brahmajaya,' 'Brahmagavi,' 'Vasa,' 'Prisni,' and 'Go,' convey ideas analogous with the customs observed in Malabar from time immemorial, I have quoted below those hymns together with their English rendering, as made by the late Ralph T. H. Griffith. All that is to be borne in mind for the clear understanding of the hymns is that the word cow is not a quadruped beast, but a metaphorical expression meaning a woman belonging to an institute of women under the power of the priestly class, for there is no evidence to believe that the Kshatriyas were cattle-lifters and that they robbed the Brahmans, their own priests, of their few cows when they had before them the

---

[46] Malabar and its Folk, by Gopal Panikar, 2nd edition, pp. 12 and 36.

precious and invaluable wealth of the early settlers of India, compared with which the value of the poor Brahmans' cows was quite insignificant. Nor is there any evidence to believe that the Brahmans gave expression to such furious and abominable threats and curses on the Kshatriyas and their kingdom for the sake of a cow or a number of cows while, on the contrary, they received as presents from the kings several cows on occasions like sacrifices and coronations of kings, as explicity stated in a number of Vedic hymns.

The hymn on the Brahmajaya (Rigveda, X. 109 and Atharvaveda, V. 17) runs as follows :—

"1. 'These first, the boundless sea, and Matarisvan, fierce-glowing fire, the strong, the Bliss-bestower, and heavenly floods, first born by holy order, exclaimed against the outrage on a Brahman.'[47]

2. King Soma first of all, without reluctance, made restitution of the Brahman's consort. Mitra and Varuna were the inviters : Agni as Hotar took her hand and led her.[48]

3. The man, her pledge, must by the hand be taken when he hath cried. She is a Brahman's consort. She stayed not for a herald to conduct her : thus is the kingdom of a ruler guarded.[49]

---

[47] The subject of the hymn, parts of which are taken from Rigveda X. 109, is the abduction by a Kshatriya of a Brahman's wife, and her subsequent restoration to her husband. The Rigveda hymn contains only seven stanzas, concluding with stanza 11 of the Atharvaveda hymn. Sea : The ocean of air. Matarisvan : probably wind. Fire : Agni. The Strong : Indra. Bliss-bestower : Soma. Outrage on a Brahman : Brahma's sin according to Sayara.—See note on stanza 5.

[48] Were the inviters : acted as interceders, or match-makers at the renewed marriage.

[49] Her pledge : her sponsor. Thus : by observing justice and causing the abducted wife to be restored. These three stanzas correspond, with slight variations, to stanzas 1-3 of the Rigveda hymn.

4 She whom they call the star with loosened tresses, descending as a misfortune on the village, the Brahman's consort, she disturbs the kingdom where hath appeared the hare with fiery flashing.[50]

5. Active in duty serves the *Brahmachari* : he is a member of the God's own body. Through him Brihaspati obtained his consort, as the gods gained the ladle brought by Soma.[51]

6. Thus spake of her those of old, seven Rishis, who sat them down to their austere devotion. Dire is a Brahman's wife led home by others ; in the supremest heaven she plants confusion.[52]

7. When infants die, untimely born, when herds of cattle waste away, when heroes strike each other dead, the Brahman's wife destroyeth them.

8. Even if ten former husbands,—none a Brahman—had espoused a dame, and then a Brahman took her hand, he is her husband, only he.

---

[50] The real cause of the misfortune attributed to meteoric influence is some disrespect shown to a Brahman's wife. Hare with fiery flashing : Some meteoric phenomenon.

[51] Rigveda, X. 109, 5. Brahmachari : a youth in the first stage of a Brahman's religious life ; a religious student. Brihaspati : that is, the injured Brahman ; Brihaspati representing the sacerdotal class. The ladle, juhum, which Professor Ludwig takes to be the lady's name : 'Juhu, O Gods, conducted home by Soma.' The meaning is obscure. A legend quoted by Sayana says that Juhu or Vak, the wife of Brihaspati who is identified with Brahma, had been deserted by her husband. The gods then consulted together as to the means of expiating his sin, and restored her to her husband. The legend has evidently grown out of the misunderstanding of the ancient hymn.

[52] Stanza 4 of Rigveda hymn. Seven Rishis : celebrated saints, sages and inspired seers of ancient times, Bharadvaja, Kasyapa, Gotama, Atri, Vasishta, Visvamitra, and Jamadagni.

9. Not Vaisya, not Rajanya, no, the Brahman is indeed her lord. This Surya in his course proclaims to the five races of mankind.[53]

10. So then the gods restored her, so men gave the woman back again. Princes who kept their promises restored the Brahman's wedded wife.[54]

11. Having restored the Brahman's wife, and freed themselves, with God's aid, from sin, they shared the fullness of the earth and won themselves extended sway.[55]

12. No lovely wife brings her dower in hundreds, rests upon his bed, within whose kingdom is detained, through want of sense, a Brahman's wife.[56]

---

[53] Rajanya: Man of the military and princely class: Kshatriya.

[54] Stanza 6 of the Rigveda hymn.

[55] Stanza 7 of the Rigveda hymn.

[56] Muir observes at the end of his translation of the non-Rigveda portion of the hymn (O. S. Texts, I., p. 281): "This hymn appears to show that, however extravagant the pretensions of the Brahmans were in other respects, they had, even at the comparatively late period when it was composed, but little regard to the purity of the sacerdotal blood, as they not only intermarried with women of their own order, or even with women who had previously lived single, but were in the habit of forming unions with the widows of Rajanyas or Vaisyas, if they did not even take possession of the wives of such men while they were alive. Even if we suppose these women to have belonged to priestly families, this would only show that it was no uncommon thing for females of that class to be married to Rajanyas or Vaisyas—a fact which would, of course, imply that the caste system was either laxly observed, or only beginning to be introduced among the Indians of the earlier Vedic age. That, agreeably to ancient tradition, Brahmans intermarried Rajanya women at the period in question, is also distinctly shown by the story of the Rishi Chyavana and Sukanya, daughter of Saryata, narrated in the Satapatha Brahmana, and quoted in my paper entitled 'Contributions to a knowledge of Vedic Mythology,' No. II, in the Journal of the Asiatic Society for 1866, p. 11 ff. See also the stories of the Rishi Syavasva, who married the daughter of King Rathaviti, as told by the commentator on Rigveda, V. 61, and given in Professor Wilson's translation, Vol. III, p. 344.

13. No broad-browed calf with wide-set ears is ever in his homestead born, within whose kingdom is detained, through want of sense, a Brahman's dame.

14. No steward, golden-necklaced, goes before the meat trays of the man within whose kingdom is detained through want of sense, a Brahman's dame.

16. No lily grows with oval bulbs, no lotus pool is in his fields, in whose dominion is detained, through senseless love, a Brahman's dame.

17. The men whose task it is to milk drain not brindled cow for him, in whose dominion is detained, through senseless love, a Brahman's dame.

18. His milch-cow doth not profit one, his draught-ox masters not the yoke, wherever, severed from his wife, a Brahman spends the mournful night.

A few words in explanation of the hymn will not be uncalled for before handling the other Vedic hymns.

Though Griffith has succeeded in making a correct and faithful translation of the hymn, he made no attempt to find out a connected meaning of the whole hymn and disposed of it by saying that it is partly obscure.

Muir attempted to explain the hymn on the supposition that Brhamans married the widows of Rajanyas and Vaisyas and even formed unions with their wives while they were alive. Evidently this supposition is inconsistent with the meaning of the word 'Brahmajaya,' Brahman's wife. Neither can a Rajanya's or Vaisya's wife be a Brahman's wife, nor a Brahman's wife the wife of the former. Also the word Brahmachari, bachelor, finds no explanation on this supposition.

On the authority of Kausika Sutra which Sayana has quoted at the heading of each of the hymns quoted here, he says that when a cow is seized (goharane), this hymn as well as the other hymns quoted here are to be recited and rites of sorcery performed. It follows therefore that Brahmajaya, Brahmagavi and Vasa are synonymous words and mean a Brahman's wife. From verse 33 of the fourth hymn of the twelfth book, where the cow is said to be the mother of a Rajanya, it is clear that the offspring of the priest and his special consort is a prince. As Sayana attributes the authorship of some of these hymns to Parasurama[57] and as the offspring of a Brahman of a chosen family and his queen consort is a bachelor king in the land of Parasurama, the States of Travancore and Cochin, it is not unreasonable to take the word Brahmachari, mentioned in verse 5 of the above hymn, to be the offspring of the couple, Brahman and Brahmajaya. The Kshatriyas and Vaisyas seem to have protested against this exclusive privilege of the priests to beget princes and prevented them from marrying or approaching the so-called Brahmajayas who, it appears, formed a set, class, or family, of women under the protection of the State, as in Travancore and Cochin. The statement, made in verse 9 of the above hymn that neither Rajanya nor a Vaisya can be a husband of the Brahmajaya, is evidently a rejoinder of the Brahmans to the protest of the Kshatriyas and Vaisyas. Both Muir and the authors of the Mahabharata, Ramayana and the Puranas in which the story of the terrible wars for the sake of a cow is narrated appear to have found the inappropriateness of these threats, imprecations, and curses with the occasional or frequent attempts of the Kshatriyas to rob the Brahmans of their quadrupeds. Hence Muir seems to have taken

---

[57] I remember to have come across this statement at the heading of one of these hymns in the German edition of the Atharvaveda. It does not appear in the Bombay edition.

the word 'go,' cow, in an extended sense of property, while the authors of the Puranas attributed supernatural powers to those animals. I think that both these attempts to explain the obscure Vedic hymns are wrong, for there is no reason to believe that though there were occasional or frequent family feuds or wars between Visvamitra and Vasishtha, between Kartaviryarjuna and Parasurama, and between a few other Kshatriyas and Brahmans, sometimes for the sake of a cow and other times for specified reasons, life and property were not so insecure among the invading Vedic Indians as to suppose that the Kshatriyas were cattle-lifters and were in the habit of robbing the Brahmans of their movable and immovable property. I think that if the interpretation I have suggested were to be accepted, none of these inconsistencies and improbabilities would crop up, and a satisfactory explanation of a hitherto inexplicable custom, prevalent in Travancore and Cochin, would be forthcoming. I do not think that the legal world is quite satisfied with the matter-of-fact explanation of the peculiar Malabar custom of inheriting the property through the female line only among the Kshatriyas, while in the rest of India it is through the male line among all classes of people.

Also in this connection Muir observes regarding the practice of remarriage of women and of intermarriage among the four classes : " That the remarriage of women was customary among the Hindus of those days is also shown by A. V., IX. 5, 27, quoted in my paper on Yama, Journal of the Royal Asiatic Society for 1865, p. 299. This latter supposition (the supposition of Brahmans taking possession of the wives of Rajanyas or Vaisyas while they were alive) derives a certain support from the emphasis with which the two verses in question (Atharvaveda, V. 17, 8, 9), assert that the Brahman was the only true husband.

Whence, it may be asked, the necessity for this strong and repeated asseveration, if the Rajanya and Vaisya husbands were still alive, and prepared to claim the restoration of their wives? The verses are, however, explicable without this supposition.

It is to be observed, however, that no mention is here made of Sudras as a class with which Brahmans intermarried. Sudras were not Aryas like the three upper classes. This distinction is recognised in the following verse of the Atharvaveda (XIX. 62, 1, 'Make me dear to gods.' From Manu (IX. 149-157 ; X. 7) it is clear that Brahmans intermarried with Sudra women, though the offspring of those marriages was degraded."

With this explanation of obscure words and phrases, let us turn our attention to the other Vedic hymns, having a wonderful cow for their subject matter :—

The hymn on Brahmagavi (A. V., XII. 5) runs as follows :—

1. 'Created[58] by toil and holy fervour, found by devotion, resting in right.

2. Invested with truth, surrounded with honour, compassed about with glory ;

3. Girt round with inherent power, fortified with faith, protected by consecration, installed at sacrifice, the world her resting place ;

4. Brahma her guide, the Brahman her lord and ruler ;

5. Of the Kshatriya who taketh to himself this Brahman's cow and oppresseth the Brahman ;

---

[58] The hymn, which is partly in prose, is a continuation of Hymn 4, inculcating, still more forcibly, the sin and danger of robbing a Brahman of his cow.

6. The glory, the heroism, and the favouring fortune depart;

7. The energy and vigour, the power and might, the speech and mental strength, the glory and duty;

8. Devotion and princely sway, kingship and people, brilliance and honour, and splendour and wealth;

9. Long life and goodly form, and name and fame, inbreathing and expiration, and sight and hearing;

10. Milk and flavour, and food and nourishment, and right and truth, and action and fulfilment, and children and cattle;

11. All these blessings of Kshatriya depart from him when he oppresseth the Brahman and taketh to himself the Brahman's cow.

12. Terrible is she, this Brahman's cow, and fearfully venomous, visibly witchcraft.

13. In her are all horrors and all deaths.

14. In her are all dreadful deeds, all slaughters of mankind.

15. This the Brahman's cow, being appropriated, holdeth bound in the fetter of death the oppresssor of the Brahman, the blasphemer of the gods.

16. A hundred-killing bolt is she; she slays the Brahman's injurer;

17. Therefore the Brahman's cow is held inviolable by the wise.

18. Running is she a thunderbolt, when driven away she is Vaisvanara.

19. An arrow when she draweth up her hooves and Mahadeva when she looketh around.

20. Sharp as a razor when beholdeth, she thundereth when she belloweth.

21. Death is she when loweth, and a fierce god when she whisketh her tail.

22. Utter destruction, when she moveth her ears this way and that, consumption when she droppeth water.

23. A missile when milking, pain in the head when milked.

24. The taking away of strength when she approacheth, a hand-to-hand fighter when roughly touched.

25. Wounding like an arrow when she is fastened by her mouth, contention when she is beaten.

26. Fearfully venomous when falling, darkness when she hath fallen down.

27. Following him, the Brahman's cow extinguisheth the vital breath of the injurer of the Brahman.

28. Hostility when being cut to pieces: Woe to children when the portions are distributed.

29. A destructive missile of gods when she is being seized; misfortune when carried away.

30. Misery while being additionally acquired, contumely and abuse while being put in the stall.

31. Poison when in agitation, fever when seasoned with condiments.

32. Sin while she is cooking, evil dream when she is cooked.

33. Uprooting when she is being turned round, destruction when she hath been turned round.

34. Discord by her smell, grief when she is being eviscerated; a serpent with poison in its fang when drawn.

35. Loss of power while sacrificially presented, humiliation when she hath been offered.

36. Wrathful Sarva while being carved, Simida[59] when cut up.

---

[59] Simida: apparently a female demon, or a disease attributed to her influence.

37. Poverty while she is being eaten, destruction when eaten.

38. The Brahman's cow when eaten cuts off the injurer of Brahmans both from this world and from the world yonder.

39. Her slaughter is the sin of witchcraft, her cutting up is a thunderbolt, her undigested grass is a secret spell.

40. Homelessness is she when denied her rights.

41. Having become flesh-eating Agni, the Brahman's cow entereth into and devoureth the oppressor of Brahmans.

42. She sunders all his members, joints and roots.

43. She cuts off relationship on the father's side and destroys maternal kinship.

44. The Brahman's cow not restored by a Kshatriya, ruins the marriages and all the kinsmen of the Brahman's oppressor.

45. She makes him houseless, homeless, childless: he is extinguished without posterity to succeed him.

46. So shall it be with the Kshatriya who takes to himself the cow of the Brahman who hath this knowledge.

47. Quickly, when he is smitten down by death, the clamorous vultures cry.

48. Quickly around his funeral fire dance women with dishevelled locks, striking the hand upon the breast and uttering their evil shriek.

49. Quickly the wolves are howling in the habitation where he lived.

50. Quickly they ask about him, what is this? What thing hath happened here?

51. Rend, rend to pieces, rend away, destroy, destroy him utterly.

52. Destroy Angirasi! the wretch who robs and wrongs the Brahmans.

53. Born of evil womb, thou witchcraft hid, for Vaisvadevi is thy name.

54. Consuming, burning all things up, the thunderbolt of spell and charm.

55. Go thou, becoming Mrityu sharp as razor's edge, pursue thy course.

56. Thou bearest off the tyrant's strength, their store of merit and their prayers.

57. Bearing off wrong, thou givest in that world to him who hath been wronged.

58. O cow, become a tracker through the curse the Brahman hath pronounced.

59. Become a bolt, an arrow through his sin, be terribly venomous.

60. O cow, break thou the head of him who wrongs the Brahmans, criminal, niggard, blasphemer of the gods.

61. Let Agni the spiteful wretch when crushed to death and slain by thee.

62. Rend, rend to bits, rend through and through, scorch and consume and burn to dust.

63. Consume thou, even from the root, the Brahman's tyrant, godlike cow!

64. That he may go from Yama's home afar into the worlds of sin.

65. So, goddess cow, go thou from him, the Brahman's tyrant, criminal, niggard, blasphemer of the gods.

66. With hundred-knotted thunderbolt, sharpened and edged with razor blades.

67. Strike off the shoulders and the head.

68. Snatch thou the hair off his head, and from his body strip the skin.

69. Tear out his sinews, cause his flesh to fall in pieces from his frame.

70. Crush thou his bones together, strike and beat the marrow out of him.

71. Dislocate all his limbs and joints.

72. From the earth let the carnivorous Agni drive him, let Vayu burn him from mid-air's broad region.

73. From heaven let Surya drive him and consume him.

Atharvaveda, XII. 4.

"1. I give the gift, shall be his word: and straightway they have bound the cow for Brahman priests who beg the boon, that bringeth sons and progeny.[60]

2. He trades and traffics with his sons, and in his cattle suffers loss who will not give the cow of gods to Rishis' children when they beg.[61]

3. They perish through a hornless cow; a lame cow sinks them in a pit. Through a maimed cow his house is burnt; an one-eyed cow destroys his wealth.

4. Fierce fever, where her droppings fall, attacks the master of the kine. So have they named her Vasa,[62] for thou art called uncontrollable.

5. The malady Viklindu[63] springs on him from ground whereon she stands, and suddenly, from fell disease perish the men on whom she sniffs.

6. Whoever twitches up her ears[64] is separated from the gods. He deems he makes a mark, but he diminishes his wealth thereby.

---

[60] On the imperative duty of giving cows to Brahmans, and the sin and danger of withholding the gift.

[61] The cow of gods: that belongs to holy priests.

[62] Vasa: a barren cow, a cow; the word being fancifully connected with Vasa, power, authority, control.

[63] Viklindu: the meaning is uncertain, perhaps dissolution, general decay.

[64] Twitches up her ears in order to brand them; and mark the cow as his own property.

7. If to his own advantage one applies the long hair of her tail, his colts, in consequence thereof, die, and the wolf destroys his calves.

8. If, while her master owneth her, a carrion crow hath harmed her hair, his young boys die thereof, decline overtakes them after fell disease.

9. What time the Dasi[65] woman throws eye on the droppings of the cow, misshapen birth arises thence, inseparable from that sin.

10. For gods and Brahmans is the cow produced when first she springs to life, hence to the priests must she be given; this they call guarding private wealth.

11. The God-created cow belongs to those who come to ask for her. They call it outrage on the priests when one retains her as his own.

12. He who withholds the cow of the gods from Rishis' sons who ask the gift is made an alien to the gods and subject to the Brahman's wrath.

13. Then let him seek another whatever his profit be in this. The cow, not given, harms a man when he denies her at their prayer.

14. Like a rich treasure stored away in safety is the Brahman's cow. Therefore men come to visit her, with whomsoever she is born.

15. So when the Brahmans come unto the cow they come unto their own. For this is her withholding, to oppress these in another life.

16. Thus after three years may she go, speaking what is not understood.[66] He, Narada! would know that cow, then Brahmans must be sought unto.

---

[65] Dasi: of barbarous or indigenous race or slave girl.

[66] Speaking what is not understood: that is giving warnings which are disregarded. Ludwig taking gada in "Avijnata gade" as coming from gadam, poison, instead of from Gada, speech, translates whose

17. Whoso call her a worthless cow, the stored-up treasure of the gods, Bhava and Sarva, both of them, move round and shoot at him.

18. The man who hath no knowledge of her udder and the teats thereof, she yields him milk with these, if he hath purposed to bestow the cow.[67]

19. If he withholds the cow they beg, she is rebellious in his stall.

Vain are the wishes and the hopes which he, withholding her, would gain.

20. The Deities have begged the cow, using the Brahman as their mouth; the man who gives her not incurs the enmity of all the gods.

22. If hundred other Brahmans beg the cow of him who owneth her, the gods have said, she, verily, belongs to him who knows the truth.

23. Whoso to others not to him who hath this knowledge, gives the cow, earth with the Deities, is hard for him to win and rest upon.

24. The Deities begged the cow from him with whom at first she was produced: Her, this one, Narada would know: with Deities he drove her forth.

25. The cow deprives of progeny and makes him poor in cattle who retains in his possession her whom Brahmans have solicited.

---

poison (deadly danger of retaining her) none hath recognized. Narada: a devarishi or Rishi of the celestial class who acts as a reporter between heaven and earth. His name is introduced as an imaginary auditor to make a warning or speech more solemn and authoritative. *Cf.* V. 19-9. The meaning of the stanza seems to be that the cow must not be retained beyond three years.

[67] The cow which the owner intends to bestow on a Brahman will give him milk without the trouble of milking her.

26. For Agni and for Soma, for Kama, Mitra and Varuna, for these the Brâhmans ask: from these is he who giveth not estranged.

27. Long as her owner hath not heard, himself, the verses,[68] let her move among his kine; when he heard, let her not make her home with him.

28. He who hath heard her verses and still makes her roam among his kine, the gods in anger rend away his life and his prosperity.

29. Roaming in many a place the cow is the stored treasure of the gods. Make manifest thy shape and form when she would seek[69] her dwelling place; then verily the cow attends to Brahman priest and their request.

31. This thought he settles in his mind, this surely goeth to the gods. Then verily the Brahman priests approach that they may beg the cow.

32. By Svadha to the Fathers, by sacrifice to the Deities, by giving them the cow, the prince doth not incur the mother's wrath.

33. The Prince's mother is the cow: so was it ordered from of old. She, when bestowed upon the priests, cannot be given back, they say.

34. As molten butter, held at length, drops down to Agni from the scoop, so falls away from Agni he who gives no cow to Brahman priests.

35. Good milker, with rice-cake[70] as calf, she in the world comes nigh to him, to him who gave her as a gift the cow grants every hope and wish.

---

[68] The verses: the holy texts recited by the Brahmans who ask for her as their fee.

[69] Would seek: jigansati (as suggested by Whitney, Index Verborum) instead of jighansati of the text.

[70] Rice-cake: Purodasa; a sacrificial cake of ground rice usually divided into pieces and offered in one or more cups.

36. In Yama's realm the cow fulfils each wish for him who gave her up; but hell, they say, is for the man who, when they beg, bestow her not.

37. Enraged against her owner roams the cow when she hath been impregnated. He deemed me fruitless, is her thought; let him be bound in snares of death.[71]

38. Whoever looking on the cow as fruitless, cooks her flesh at home, Brihaspati compels his sons and children to beg.

40. The animal is happy when it is bestowed upon the priests; but happy is the cow when she is made a sacrifice to gods.

41. Narada chose the terrible vilipti[72] out of all the cows which the gods formed and framed when they had risen up from sacrifice.

42. The gods considered her in doubt whether she were a cow or not, Narada spake of her and said, The veriest cow of cows is she.

---

[71] Prof. Haug observes in his note: "That cows were killed at the time of receiving most distinguished guests is stated in the Smritis. But, as Sayana observes, which entirely agrees with the opinions held now-a-days, this custom belongs to former Yugas (periods of the world). Thence the word Goghna, *i.e.*, cow-killer, means in the more ancient Sanskrit books 'a guest' (see the commentators on Panini 3,4,73): for the reception of a highly respected guest was the death of the cow of the house." According to Apastamba's Aphorisms on the Sacred Law of the Hindus, the Snataka or student who has completed his course of religious study, when he speaks of a cow that is not a milch-cow is not to say 'she is not a milch-cow' but 'But this is a cow which will become a milch-cow.' See Sacred Books of the East, Vol. II, p. 95.

Fruitless: Vehatam; a cow which habitually miscarries, and which may therefore be slaughtered 'when a king or another man deserves high honour' is to be received (Aitareya Brahmana, I. 15).

[72] Vilipti: literally, besmeared or anointed.

43. How many cows, O Narada, knowest thou, born among mankind I ask thee who dost know, of which must none who is no Brahman eat?

44. Vilipti, cow, and she who drops no second calf, Brihaspati! Of these none but a Brahman should eat if he hope for eminence.

45. Homage, O Narada, to thee who hast quick knowledge of the cows. Which of these is the direst, whose withhelding bringeth death to man?

46. Vilipti, O Brihaspati, cow, mother of no second calf; of these none, not a Brahman should eat if he hope for eminence.

47. Threefold are kine, Vilipti, cow, the mother of no second calf: these one should give to priests, and he will not offend Prajapati.

48. This, Brahmans! is your sacrifice: thus should one think when he is asked, what time they beg from him the cow fearful in the withholder's house.

49. He gave her not to us, so spake the gods, in anger, of the cow. With these same verses they addressed Bheda,[73] this brought him to his death.

50. Solicited by Indra, still Bheda refused to give this cow. In strife for victory the gods destroyed him for that sin of his.

51. The men of evil counsel who advised refusal of the cow, miscreants through their foolishness, are subjected to Indra's wrath.

52. They who seduce the owner of the cow and say, bestow her not, encounter through their want of sense the missile shot by Rudra's hand.

---

[73] Bheda: nothing further appears to be known of this man who refused to give his cow to Indra.

53. If in his home one cooks the cow, sacrificed or not sacrificed, wronger of gods and Brahmans, he departs, dishonest, from the world.

1. The gods, O Prince, have not bestowed this cow on thee to eat thereof. Seek not, Rajanya, to devour the Brahman's cow which none may eat.[74]

2. A base Rajanya, spoiled at dice, and ruined by himself, may eat the Brahman's cow, and think, to-day and not to-morrow, let me live!

3. The Brahman's cow is like a snake, charged with dire poison, clothed with skin. Rajanya! bitter to the taste is she, and none may eat of her.

4. She takes away his strength, she mars his splendour, she ruins everything like fire enkindled. That man drinks poison of the deadly serpent who counts the Brahman's cow as mere food to feed him.

5. Whoever smites him, deeming him awakening blasphemer, coveting his wealth through folly, Indra sets fire alight within his bosom. He who acts thus is loathed by earth and heaven.

6. No Brahman must be injured, safe as fire from him who loves himself. For Soma is akin to him and Indra guards him from the curse.

7. The fool who eats the Brahman's food and thinks it pleasant to the taste, eats, but can never digest, the cow that bristles with a hundred barbs.

8. His voice is an arrow's neck, his tongue a bowstring, his windpipes fire-enveloped heads of arrows, with these the Brahman pierces through blasphemers, with god-sped bows that quell the hearts within them.

---

[74] A. V., V. 18. The hymn declares the wickedness and ruinous consequences of oppressing and robbing the Brahmans.

9. Keen arrows have the Brahmans, armed with missiles; the shaft, when they discharge it, never faileth. Pursuing him with fiery zeal and anger, they pierce the foeman even from a distance.

10. They who, themselves ten hundred, were the rulers of a thousand men, the Vaitahavyas.[75]

11. The cow, indeed, when she was slain, overthrew those Vaitahavyas, who cooked the last she-goat that remained of Kesaraprabandha's[76] flock.

12. One and a hundred[77] were the folk, those whom the earth shook off[78] from her: when they had wronged the Brahman's race they perished inconceivably.

13. Among mankind the gods' despiser moveth; he hath drunk poison, naught but one is left him, who wrongs the kinsman of the gods, the Brahman, gains not the sphere to which the Fathers travelled.

14. Agni, in sooth, is called our guide, Soma is called our next-of-kin. Indra quells him who curses us. Sages know well that this is so.

15. Prince! like a poisoned arrow, like a deadly snake, O Lord of Kine! dire is the Brahman's arrow; he pierces his enmies therewith.

---

[75] Vaitahavyas: a tribe or people in the north; literally, descendants or people of Vitahavya. A Rishi of this name appears to be mentioned in Rigveda, VI. 15, a hymn ascribed to him by Sayana. The Vaitahavyas are mentioned in the Anusasana parva of the Mahabharata, 1952-1977, where they are said to have been defeated and slain in battle.

[76] Kesaraprabandha: I can find no other mention of this woman.

[77] One and a hundred: an unlucky number used with reference to phases of disease, modes of death and the like.

[78] The earth shook off: in horror at their wickedness.

1. The sons [79] of Vitahavya, [80] the Srinjayas waxed exceeding strong. They well-nigh touched the heavens, but they wronged Bhrigu and were overthrown.

2. When men pierced Brihatsaman [81] through, the Brahman, son of Angiras, the ram with teeth in both his jaws, the sheep, devoured their progeny.

3. If men have spat upon or shot their rheum upon a Brahman, they sit [82] in the middle of a stream running with blood, devouring hair.

4. While yet the Brahman's cow which men are dressing quivers in her throes, she mars the kingdom's splendour; there no vigorous hero springs to life.

5. Terrible is her cutting up; her bitter flesh is cast away. And it is counted sin among the fathers if her milk is drunk.

6. If any king who deems himself mighty would eat a Brahman up, rent and disrupted is that realm where in a Brahman is oppressed.

7. She [83] grows eight-footed, and four-eyed, four-eared, four-jawed, two-faced, two-tongued, and shatters down the kingdom of the man who doth Brahman wrong.

---

[79] The subject of the hymn A. V., V. 19 is wickedness and ruinous consequences of oppressing, robbing or insulting a Brahman.

[80] Vitahavya: see v. 18, 1.

Srinjayas: a people in the north. Bhrigu: a Rishi regarded as the ancestor of the ancient race of Bhrigus who are frequently mentioned in the Rigveda in connection with Agni, and who are specially associated with the Atharvaveda hymns. The story of the overthrow, of the Vaitahavyas is told in the Mahabharata Anusasanaparva, 1952-1977, but Bhrigu is there said to have given refuge to the King Vitahavya after his defeat.

[81] Brihatsaman: the name of this descendant of the ancient Rishi Angiras does not recur in the Veda, and his story is not mentioned elsewhere.

[82] They sit: after death in the internal regions.

[83] She: the cow.

8. As water swamps a leaky ship, so ruin overflows that realm. Misfortune smites the realm wherein a Brahman suffers scathe and harm.

9. The very trees repel the man, and drive him from their sheltering shade, whoever claims, O Narada, [84] the treasure that a Brahman owns.

10. That wealth, King Varuna hath said, is poison by the gods prepared. None hath kept watch to guard his realm who hath devoured a Brahman's cow.

11. Those nine and ninety [85] people whom the earth shook and cast away from her, when they had wronged the Brahman race, were ruined inconceivably.

12. Oppressor of the Brahmans ; thus the gods have spoken and declared, the step-effacing wisp [86] they bind upon the dead shall be thy couch.

13. Oppressor of the Brahmans! tears wept by the man who suffers wrong, these are the share of water which the gods have destined to be thine.

14. The share of water which the gods have destined to be thine, is that, oppressor of the priest! wherewith men lave the corpse and wet the beard. [87]

15. The rain of Mitra-Varuna falls not on him who wrongs the priest. To him no command brings success; he wins no friend to do his will.

---

[84] Narada: a Devarishi or saint of the celestial class who often comes down to earth to report what is going on in heaven and return with his account of what is being done on earth. His name is introduced to make the warning more solemn and impressive.

[85] Those nine and ninety: *cf.* V.18, 12 where they are said to have been a hundred and one.

[86] The step effacing wisp: obliterating the footsteps of the dead on his journey to the other world, so that death may not reach the surviving kinsmen by the same path.

[87] The beard: to be shaved off before cremation.

1. How, terrible in might, hast thou here spoken to the great god, how to the gold-hued Father? Thy mind watched, greedy Varuna, to recover the brindled cow thou hadst bestowed as guerdon.[88]

2. Not through desire do I revoke my present: I bring this brindled cow to contemplate her. Now by what lore, by what, inherent nature, knowest thou all things that exist, Atharvan.[89]

3. Truly I am profound in wisdom, truly I know by nature all existing creatures. No Dasa by his greatness, not an Arya, may violate the law that I will establish.[90]

4. None, self-dependent Varuna! existeth wiser than thou or sager by his wisdom. Thou knowest well all these created beings: even the man of wondrous powers fears thee.

5. O self-dependent Varuna, wise director, thou knowest verily all generations. What is, unerring one! beyond this region? What more remote than that which is most distant?

6. One thing there is beyond this air, and something beyond that one most hard to reach remotest. I, Varuna, who know, to thee declare it. Let churls be mighty in the lower regions. Let Dasas sink into the earth beneath them.[91]

---

[88] This curious hymn contains A. V., V. 11, a dialogue between the primeval priest Atharvan and Varuna about the possession of a wonderful brindled cow. The god has bestowed the cow upon the priest, and now retracts his gift. Atharvan remonstrates. Atharvan speaks. Spoken: declared thy promise to give me the cow. The great god: heaven. The gold hued father: the sun.

[89] Varuna replies. To contemplate her: or, to count her with the rest of the herd.

[90] In this and the two following stanzas Atharvan speaks.

[91] Varuna replies: Beyond the air is heaven, and beyond that is infinity.

7. Many reproaches, Varuna, dost thou utter against the misers who revoke their presents. Be not thou added to that crowd of niggards: let not men call thee an illiberal giver. [92]

8. Let not men call me an illiberal giver. I give thee back the brindled cow, O singer. Attend, in every place where men inhabit, with all thy powers, the hymn that tells my praises. [93]

9. Let hymns of praises ascend to thee, uplifted in every place of human habitation. But give me now the gift thou hast given. Thou art my friend for ever firm and faithful. [94]

10. One origin, [95] Varuna ! one bond unites us: I know the nature of that Common kinship. I give thee now the gift that I retracted. I am thy friend for ever firm and faithful.

11. God, giving life unto the god who lauds me, sage, strengthener of the sage who sings my praises. [96] Thou, self-dependent Varuna! hast begotten the kinsman of the gods, our sire Atharvan. On him bestow most highly lauded riches. Thou art our friend high over all, our kinsman.

The Sachi Paulomi hymn of the Rigveda (X. 159) in which a queen is made to speak in a tone of exultation of her own and of her daughter's imperial sway seems also

---

[92] Atharvan speaks.

[93] Varuna speaks.

[94] Atharvan speaks this stanza and the first hemistich of 10. Ever firm and faithful Saptapadas, literally 'having taken seven steps' by which an alliance or a marriage is confirmed.

[95] One origin: the ancient Rishis frequently assert their kinship with the gods, as sons of Dyaus or Father Heaven. Varuna speaks the second hemistich and the first of the following stanza.

[96] Unto the god: the priest Atharvan. The second and third lines are spoken by the poet of the hymn.

to contain a clear allusion to the institute of queens. The hymn runs as follows :—

"1. Yon Sun hath mounted up, and this my happy fate hath mounted high.

I, knowing this, as conqueror have won my husband for my own.

I am the banner and the head, a mighty arbitress am I.

2. I am victorious and my lord shall be submissive to my will.

My sons are slayers of the foe, my daughter is a ruling queen.

3. I am victorious : over my lord ; my song of triumph is supreme.

Oblation, that which Indra gave and thus grew glorious and most high,—

4. This I have offered, O ye gods, and rid me of each rival wife destroyer of rival wife, sole spouse, victorious conqueror.

5. The others' glory have I seized as it were the wealth of weaker dames.

6. I have subdued as conqueror these rival wives these my fellow wives,

That I may hold imperial sway over this hero and the folk."

It should be noted here how the queen is made to speak of her sons as being merely slayers of the foe while her daughter is represented as a ruling queen. She is also made to speak of her husband as holding a subordinate position in the kingdom over which her power was supreme. It is true that his hymn can also be explained on the supposition of the existence of a hereditary monarchy running on the line of male issues and of princesses being wedded to a ruling king of a different state, and of plurality of wives in the royal harem. Still it cannot be denied that this hymn and its peculiar expressions can also find a ready explanation on the hypothesis of the institution of Brahmajayas or queens, in the light of which her imperial sway over the folk and over her husband can be taken as a fact instead of a boast.

The other words which appear to have been misunderstood by our epic writers and which gave rise to a number of inconsistent and exaggerated statements and stories are Brahma and Praja. The word Brahma in the Vedas meant a priest as well as a god, while praja denoted one's own children or people at large. The Epic-writers took the word Brahma in the sense of a god and praja in the sense of children. Accordingly such Vedic expressions as 'Manu was Brahma's son' and 'Prajas were Manavas' seem to have been taken by them to mean that Manu was the Creator's own son, and that the people were Manu's children, while the real sense was that Manu was the Chief Priest's son and that the people were Manu's subjects when he was first elected as a king. Likewise expressions such as 'Sagara had sixty-thousand prajas or people under him' seem to have meant for them that Sagara had sixty-thousand sons.

The story of Krishnadvaipayana begetting on the queens Amba and Ambalica, Dhritarashtra and Pandu to rule over the Kuru kingdom can also find a satisfactory explanation in the light of the institution of queens.

I may therefore conclude that the priestly class of the Aryan invaders of India established an institution of queens and reserved to themselves the right of begetting on them a ruling king and warrior soldiers to protect and defend the kingdom, the king and the soldiers being compelled to observe a celebate life and having no ruling powers over the priestly class. Consequent on the desire of the Kshatriyas to set up a hereditary monarchy with right of marriage for the Kshatriyas also, a Civil War ensued between the Brahmans and the Kshatriyas and ended in a triumph for the latter. It is also probable that as Divodasa, Purukirtsa, Trasadasyu and others are found mentioned in the Vedas as hereditary monarchs, there were some states which set up hereditary monarchy at the very start with no institution of queens, while in others that institution was amicably settled to terminate in hereditary, though in its pristine Vedic form it is still found to linger in the states of Travancore and Cochin. As there is reason to believe that the elected queens were of Aryan descent and the begetting priests also were true Aryans, it follows that many of our Kshatriya kings and especially those of Travancore and Cochin are kings with true Aryan blood running in their veins, while the same cannot be said of all the Brahmans owing to their connection in some cases with Sudra women by marriage, the offspring of this union having been allowed to exercise the functions of Brahmans.[97]

---

[97] Latyayana Srauta, IX. 2, 6.

LECTURE IV

THE PEOPLE'S ASSEMBLY

From time immemorial, the Aryans as a race seem to have exhibited an innate desire to settle their social, religious, or political questions in an assembly of their own. The Greeks had their Areopagus, the Romans their Curia; and the Anglo-Saxons their Witanagemot. Likewise the Aryans of India had their own Sabha or Samiti. The other names given to a Sabha are Janata, and Parishad. The words Sabha, Samiti and Janata are Vedic and Parishad is the word commonly used during the Sutra-period. Brihaspati quoted in the Vyavaharakanda of Parasaramadhava (pp. 18, 19) mentions four kinds of assemblies; one called the immovable assembly in a town or a village, a second termed movable assembly, perhaps of learned men moving from place to place, a third [98] called chartered committee with a presiding superintendent and a fourth [99] styled ordered assembly with the king to preside over its deliberations. Bhrigu, quoted in the same work (p. 19), mentions some other minor assemblies of particular castes. He says that wild tribes have their own assemblies, the merchants their own guild, the army its own assembly composed of soldiers, the villagers their own, the townspeople their own, and the Srenis or washermen and other eighteen kinds of low caste people have their special assemblies. These classes, whether a Gana, composed of a number of families, or a congregation of heretics, or a corporation of Brahmans or an assemblage

[98] Mudritadhyakshasamyukta p. 19.

[99] Rajayukta cha Sastrita, p. 19.

of people of different castes and creeds, are termed Vargins and are said to have their own assemblies. Apart from these minor assemblies, there seems to have been in each stage during the Sutra period a grand assembly consisting of families, elders, government officers and the king himself.[100]

It is probable that even during the Vedic period there were in addition to the grand assembly of the State minor assemblies formed by each class for settling its own social or religious questions. The grand assembly with the king as its president seems to have been the final authority on all questions. According to Narada quoted in Parasara-madhava Vyavahara (p. 32) the gradation of appellate authorities is as follows :—(1) families (kulani), (2) Srenis or washermen and other eighteen low-castes, (3) Gana, or congregation of families and (4) the anointed king himself. Even now only such social, religious, or political questions as villagers find it difficult to satisfactorily settle in their own village assemblies are brought before criminal or civil courts for settlement. It is probable that even during the Vedic period the same practice of settling their affairs either by themselves or by the king in his assembly was followed by the Aryans. It is improbable, if not impracticable, that each of the many villagers that constituted a kingdom of the Vedic period was compelled to go to the grand assembly in the capital town of the king for the settlement of its questions. It is therefore likely that the numerous references[101] to sabhas or assemblies found the Vedic literature are not merely to the single king's

---

[100] Kulani Kulikaschaiva niyukta nripatishatha. Parasaramadhaviya Vyavahara, p. 19.

[101] Rig. VI. 28, 6; VIII. 4, 9, X. 34. 6; VI; 71, 10, A. V. 31, 6; VII. 12, 2; VIII. 10, 5; XIX. 55, 6. Tai. S. I. 6, 7. Tai. Br. I. 1, 10, 6. Sat. Br. II. 3, 2, 8; V. 3, 1, 10. Vaj. S. III. 45; XVI. 24: XX. 17, etc.

assembly in the capital town, but to minor village assemblies also.

With regard to membership of assemblies, there seems to have been no restriction whatever. Whether old or young, educated or uneducated, all seem to have had free admittance into the assembly whenever it was convened. It it also probable that there was no question of quorum, but the presence of every villager was necessary to make the assembly fully authoritative. Even now it is an accepted custom with villagers in Mysore to ascertain whether every villager is present in the meeting before authorising the assembly to take up the question at issue into consideration. The educated and the aged are respected by the uneducated and the young merely by granting to the former seats of honour or by seating themselves at a respectable distance, though on the same mat or carpet. Though the right of discussion and decision is as a matter of fact granted by a common consent to the educated and the aged, no man, whether ignorant or young, is denied the right of expressing his view, merely on account of his ignorance or youth. Even during the times of Charaka, the author of Charaka-samhita, the same procedure of convening meetings with men of all grades and positions seems to have been in vogue. This is what Charaka says about the various kinds of assemblies prevalent at his time :—

" Without doubt, the assembly may be of two kinds : (1) an assembly of men endued with knowledge and wisdom, (2) an assembly of men that are ignorant. Though principally of two kinds, it may be of three kinds according to difference of causes noted below :— (1) an assembly that is friendly, (2) an assembly that is indifferent and (3) an assembly that is already committed to one side.[102] As the Krishnayajurveda (II. 2, 2) has prescribed some sacrificial spells for avoiding nervousness in an assembly and for the acquisition of the power of eloquence, it follows that assemblies were convened on a grand scale and that no one was denied the right of expressing his views in the assembly. The priests, representing the educated, the nobility representing the agricultural and the trading class were all present there. As questions of election and banishment of kings and of restoration of banished kings were discussed in the assembly, it is doubtful whether kings attended it or not. If it were a rule that the king should attend it, it would follow that he attended it as its head to preside over its deliberations. But as questions of election and restoration of a king cropped up as subjects of discussion only when there was no king in the kingdom, some one else, a distinguished priest or a noble, might volunteer himself as its president for the time being; and when the question of the banishment of the tyrannical king was the subject of discussion in the assembly, the tyrant himself might stay away from it in the interests of his own personal safety or dignity. There is however no reliable reference found in the Vedas about the king's attendance in the assembly as its president. The Rigvedic references to the presence of a Raja in the midst of an assembly (IX. 92, 6, and X. 97, 6) can be taken to mean either as the presence of a noble in the midst of an assembly or as the presence of a king in festal assemblies or congregations, or battles, as interpreted by Sayana in (IX. 92, 6). On no account the two passages can be taken to mean that the king attended the assembly as its president. Moreover as there are Vedic passages enjoining certain charms and spells for

[102] Vimanasthana. Chapter 8, 17.

the acquisition of the power of eloquence so as to secure unanimity in the assembly, it appears that the right of addressing the assembly was vested in no one, but was given to any one who volunteered himself to undertake it. Similar is the custom in vogue in villages even now. The best speaker or pedagogue is even now allowed to address the people and carry the day as he might. The same form of pedagogy which is recommended by Charaka for vanquishing an opponent in disputation prevails even now in the assemblies of villages, and seems to have prevailed also during the Vedic period. This is what Charaka says :—

"An opponent that is weak in the Scriptures should be vanquished with citations of lengthy aphorisms. An opponent should be vanquished by the use of phrases fraught with words, the sense of which is too difficult to understand. An opponent that is unable to understand the words he hears should be vanquished by reciting lengthy aphorisms full of difficult words."[103]

That such was the form of debate in the Vedic period is confirmed by the various kinds of sacrifices prescribed in the Vedas for the attainment of debating power in assemblies.[104] It is likely therefore that no king ever presided in the assembly of the people, but that only he consented to do or undo anything, as required by the unanimous desire of the assembly. That he was bound to act up to the unanimous decision of the assembly is confirmed by the following hymn of the Atharvaveda: (VI. 88, 3) :—

"Firm, never to be shaken, crush thy foemen, under thy feet lay those who strive against thee. One-minded,

---

[103] Vimanasthana, Chapters 8, 17.

[104] A. V. V. 31, 6.

true to thee be all the regions; faithful to thee, the firm, be this assembly."[105]

Drinking of Sura, an intoxicating liquor, seems to have been a common custom with men going to Sabha or assembly. This is confirmed by the following passage of the Atharvaveda :—

"He, (the Vratya) went away to the people. Meeting, assembly, army and wine followed him. He who hath this knowledge becomes the dear home of meeting, assembly, army and wine."[106]—(A. V. XV. 9.)

It follows therefore that eloquent talk and wild and violent disputation was a common feature of the debate in an assembly, perhaps often leading to broils. But there is evidence to believe that assembly-halls were considered so sacred that while in the assembly, even a criminal was sure of his personal safety. This is confirmed by the following passage of the Rigveda (I. 31, 6) :—

"Agni, thou savest in the assembly when pursued, even him, O farseeing one! who walks in evil ways."

To win glory by exhibiting extraordinary power of eloquence in the assembly seems to have been the highest ambition of men even in those days. Among the various blessings hoped for, the birth of a son fit for the assembly is one, as clearly expressed in the following grand benedictory passage of the Yajurveda (VII. 5, 18) :—

"In this preisthood may a Brahman be born of spiritual glory; in this kingdom may a prince be born, an archer, a hero, and a great chariot-fighter; a milk cow, a draught ox, a swift racer (horse), a prolific woman, a victorious warrior, a youth fit for the assembly (sabhya). To

---

[105] See Vedic Index, Vol. II, p. 431 :—concord between the king and his assembly was essential for his prosperity.

[106] *Cf.* Rig. VII, 86, 6; VIII. 2, 12; 21, 14; A. V. XIV. 1, 35-36.

this sacrificer may a hero be born. May Parjanya rain for us whensoever we desire. May our plants ripen with fruits. May union and peace be ours."

One of the Rigvedic hymns conveys the same idea (I. 40, 5-6) :—

"Now Brahmanaspati speaks forth aloud the solemn hymn of praise,

Wherein Indra, Varuna, Mitra, Aryaman, the gods have made their dwelling place.

May we in holy assemblies, O gods, recite that hymn, peerless, that brings felicity.

If you, O heroes, graciously accept this word.

May it obtain all bliss from you."

In this connection the following Atharvavedic prayers for power of debate and of voice are also interesting :—

1. Let not the enemy win the cause! strong and predominant art thou.

Refute my adversary's speech. Render them dull and flat, O! plant.

2. The strong winged bird discovered thee, the bird unearthed thee with his snout.

Refute my adversary's speech. Render them dull and flat, O! plant.

3. Ye, Indra laid thee on his arm to cast the Asuras to the ground.

Refute my adversary's speech. Render them dull and flat, O! plant.

5. With this, I overcome my foes as Indra overcame the wolves.

Refute my.........

7. Indra, defeat the speech of him who meets us with hostility.

Comfort us with power and might. Make me superior in debate." A. V. II, 27.

"1. Mine be the glory in the hill, in vales, in cattle, and in gold,

Mine be the sweetness that is found in nectar and in flowing wine.

2. With your delicious honey balm me, Asvins, lords of splendid light!

That clear and resonant may be the voice I utter to mankind, assembly.

3. In me be strength, in me be fame, in me the power of sacrifice.

Prajapati establish this in me as firm as light in heaven." A. V. VI. 69.

Decision on questions seems to have been arrived at by obtaining vote of the majority as prevalent later at the time of Chanakya,[107] and disputes about field by securing the unanimous consent of the people assembled, any jarring note of dissent being hushed up by the persuasive power of eloquence of the speaker or speakers.

This is proved by the following hymns of the Atharvaveda :—

"1. Agree and be united : let your minds be all of one accord.

Even as the gods of ancient days, unanimous, await their share.

2. The Rede is common, common the assembly, common the law, so be their thoughts united.

I offer up your general oblation ! together entertain one common purpose.

3. *One and the same be your resolve,* be all your hearts in harmony.

One and the same be all your minds that all may happily consent." (A. V. VI. 64.)

---

[107] Artha. III. 9.

"1. In *conc rd* may Prajapati's daughters, Sabha and Samiti, both protect me.

May every man I meet respect and aid me. Fair be my words, O' Fathers ! at the meetings.

2. We know thy name, O conference : thy name is interchange of talk.

Let all the company who join the conference *agree with me.*

3. Of the men seated here, I make the splendour and the lore mine own.

Indra make me conspicuous in all this gathered company.

4. Whether your thoughts are turned away or bound and fostered here or there,

We draw them hitherward again : let your mind firmly rest on me." (A.V. VII. 12.)

Since the word Sabha is a name given to the gambling-hall where the favourite, though ruinous, game of dice was played at, it is probable that assemblies also met there whenever necessary. In villages having no gambling houses, meetings seem to have been held in temples, or places of fireworship built for common use or in private houses with such common apartments.[108] Sabhya and Sabhika are two modern terms, of which the latter denotes a member of the gambling company. Sabhapathi, lord of the assembly, seems to have denoted a mediator or president.

Though there is however no Vedic record as to the way in which business was done in the assembly, still some hint may be gathered about this point from what Brihaspati and other Smriti writers have spoken of it at a later period. Regarding the ten essential constituents

---

[108] Artha, III. 8 ; Vedic Index, Vol. II, p. 426.

of an assembly Brihaspati is said to have laid down as follows :—

"(1) The king, (2) the appointed members of the assembly, (3) the Smritis, (4) the accountant, (5) the writer, (6) gold, (7) fire, (8) water, and (9 & 10) witnesses of the two parties. Of these, the king is to decide; the members of the assembly to examine; the smritis to furnish the law, gold and fire for taking oaths upon, water for the thirsty, the the accountant to count, the writer to take down the statements and the witnesses to confirm the case."[109]

Of these, the king and the writer may be omitted, as no king seems to have attended the assembly and no writing was known in those days. That the rest were all there, as constituents, is a point that need not be doubted.

While this statement of Brihaspati determines to some extent the procedure of business done in the assembly, there is a good deal of uncertainty as to the nature of subjects that were discussed in the assembly still it is not, however, difficult to guess at the truth from internal and external evidences. Since special mention is made not merely of election and banishment of kings as pointed out elsewhere, it follows that those questions were thoroughly discussed and decided in the peoples' assembly. Though Macdonell and Keith admit that there are clear references to kings being expelled from their realms, and their efforts to recover their sovereignty, they hesitate to accept Zimmer's opinion that while the Vedic monarchy was sometimes hereditary, as is indeed shown by several cases where the descent can be traced, yet in others the monarchy was elective, though it is not clear whether the selec-

109 Parasaramadhava Vyavahara, p. 25.

tion *by the people* was between the members of the royal family only or extended to members of all the noble clans.[110]

I do not see any reason for this doubt on their part when according to the express text of the Krishna Yajurveda[111] the elected king is declared to be the sovereign not of all the people, the clergy, the nobility and common folk, but merely of the two latter classes. The text runs as follows :—

" This is your king, O Bharatas, but Soma is the king of us, Brahmans." (I. 8, 10.)

Here the priests seem to be the king-makers or Raja-krits, as they are called in two of the Atharvavedic hymns (IV. 22, 3 & 5 ; VIII. 7, 6). Thus when the king-makers elect a king after obtaining the unanimous consent of the nobility and the common people, as stated in the other hymns of the Atharvaveda quoted above (I. 9 ; III. 4 ; IV. 22) and declare that the elected and anointed king is not to be considered to be the king of the Brahmans also, it follows that the constitution was partly oligarchical and partly monarchical and that the voice of the priests on the election and retention of a king was supreme in the people's assembly.

The other questions that seem to have formed the subjects of discussion in the assembly are[112] war,[113] peace,[114] disputes about land,[115] recovery of debts, [116] cheating at

---

110 Vedic Index, Vol. I. p. 211.

111 Yajus, I. 8, 10.

112 A. V., VI. 75, 103.

113 A. V., VII. 52.

114 Krishna Yajus, II. 2. 1.

115 A. V., VI. 117.

116 A. V., VI. 118 and 119.

play,[117] inheritance,[118] taxation,[119] abduction of women,[120] protection of men and cattle,[121] cattle stealing,[122] distribution of war-spoils,[123] currency or coins of money such as Krishnal, Nishka, and Satamana,[124] trade and tolls (sulka),[125] crimes such as theft, assault, and murder.

Apart from these questions which are all referred to directly or indirectly in the Vedas, many of the questions that obtained cognisance in the civil and criminal courts of the Sutra period seem also to have engaged the attention of the peoples' assembly of the Vedic period. Among the several duties assigned in the Sutras to the kings' assembly for decision, the following seem appropriate for the Vedic period also[126] :—

(1) Destruction of fruit trees.

(2) Falsification of weights and measures.

(3) Provision for the wives of soldiers slain in battle.

(4) Exemption of Brahmans and widows from taxation.

(5) Maintenance of the poor, eunuchs, and madmen.

(6) Punishment of false witnesses.

It should however be noted that neither the veracity of social, religious and political questions discussed in the assembly nor the way in which the decision was arrived at is of so much importance as the question of the constitution of the government machinery itself. We know for certain

---

117 Krishna Yajus, II. 6, 1.

118 A. V. III. 29.

119 A. V. V. 17.

120 A. V. VI. 107.

121 Rig. I. 118.

122 Rig. II. 111.

123 Satapata Br. XII, 7, 2, 13 ; XIII, 1, 1, 47, etc.

124 Tai. Sa. III. 1, 2. 1.

125 Vaj. Samhita XXX. 5.

126 Vasishtha and Bodhayana : Bühler's Translation.

that the two important elements that constituted the government of the Vedic period were the assembly and the king. Of these two, the assembly must have been more important than the king who evidently was at the mercy of the former. As pointed out already, it was the assembly that managed the affairs of the kingdom during the periods of interregnum due to death or banishment of kings. Even during the later periods of hereditary monarchy it is the assembly of ministers that invariably assisted the king in all matters concerning the State. While during the Vedic period the assembly evidently held a permanent place in the constitution, it occupied a subordinate place in the Sutra period.

LECTURE V.

THE DUTIES AND PREROGATIVES OF THE KINGS AND PRIESTS.

It may be stated without the fear of contradiction that history of the world means the history of the play of intellect. It is the intelligent few that rule the world and are the causes of its progress or deterioration. It is they that shape the policy of governments and give it this or that name to please the vanity and whimsical notions of the times. So long as the intelligent few are altruistic in their acts towards the people that are in social intercourse with them, they are respected and admired. When they act either in their own self-interests or against the selfish or unselfish interests of the powerful or of a body of the people, they begin to be hated by the latter. When the intelligent few form themselves into a separate class or caste and begin to be hated for their apparent selfish interests, the feeling of hatred is in the long run converted into a permanent class or caste hatred, though the cause of that feeling may have long died away.

What at a later period appear as forms of selfish interests originate themselves at first as deserved privileges and rights granted and enjoyed in honour of the intellectual superiority, protective capacity or governing skill. The chief, the king, the medicine man, the religious priest with his assumed power of interpreting the signs of the heavens and his spells, incantations and sacrificial exploits are first admired and respected for their power in war, in governing, in curing diseases, and in exorcising devils and averting calamities of hidden origin, and are granted gifts. The families of these men continue to enjoy those privileges even on the death of the heroes and the priests with whom the rights originated. In the long run the rights become mere toys with no merit to render them deserved, no matter whether the claimants of the rights are individuals or a class of people.

This is what has happened with the prerogatives of Indian priestly class, which earned its privileges in honour of its superior intellect. The rights and privileges of the king, on the other hand, began to increase in proportion to the growth of his governing duties. The duties of the kings, whether hereditary or elected for life, were very few at first while those of the priests were many. While the king was expected to confine his attention to the protective and defensive measure of the kingdom, it was the priest with whom the power to help the kings by the performance of necessary sacrifices and spells was believed to rest. It was his sacrifice that averted droughts by causing timely rains. It was his sacrifice that ensured victory to the king over his enemy. It was his sacrifice that brought in a plentiful harvest. It was his sacrifice and medical amulet that introduced concord between the king and the people. In short there was no public or private activity that is not attended with a sacrificial performance. His memory was so strong that he remembered a number of suitable prayers which he alone knew to interpret. He alone knew to perform sacrifices so correctly as to ensure success. His failure to achieve expected success was due to insufficiency of the sacrifices. Thus he was a god incarnate to the people of his times. Even so late as the time of Chanakya, the duty of a king it was to employ a chief priest well learned in the Vedas and experienced in the performance of various kinds of sacrifices.

The other kinds of service which the priestly class rendered to the king and his people in addition to the religious and sacrificial services and which made the privileges granted to it highly deserved in the eyes of the people are educational, spiritual, and ministerial. As repositories of knowledge, both secular and sacred, the priests were justly looked upon as persons well qualified to impart knowledge of all kinds to those who were inclined to aquire them. Their abodes not merely in towns and villages but also in hermitages situated on the banks of rivers in forests seem to have been frequented by all sorts of people, inclusive of kings. Their hermitages and other settlements seem to have been regarded so sacred as to insure safety of person and security of property. Even kings defeated, driven out and chased from the battlefields seem to have found in the hermitages a safe shelter from their bloodthirsty enemies. This is confirmed by the story of Kings Sudarsana and Suratha narrated in IV. 16, 17 and V. 32 of the Devibhagavata. The story of Sudarsana is as follows :—Dhruvasandhi, son of Pushpa and King of the Kosalas had two sons, one called Sudarsana by his first wife Manorama and another named Satrujit by Lilavati. Dhruvasandhi died while hunting. A battle ensued between Virasena, King of Kalinga, and Yudhajit, King of Ujjaini, each being interested in securing the throne of Dhruvasandhi to his own nephew, Sudarsana and Satrujit respectively. Then apprehending danger from Yudhajit, Manoranma with her young son fled to the hermitage of Bharadvaja and lived there in peace till her son grew old and received his education in the Vedas, politics and military art from Bharadvaja himself so as to recover his lost kingdom. So he did to the satisfaction of his mother.

Likewise, Suratha, an ancient king, driven out from his kingdom by his enemies, sought refuge in the hermitage of Sumedhas and with his assistance recovered his kingdom.

The birth and growth of Sagara in the hermitage of Aurva on the death of his father Bahu defeated and driven out from his kingdom by the Haihayas and the Talajanghas is another instance of the indispensable protective care and shelter which kings in exile sought and received from the priestly class.[127]

It seems to have been a unique spectacle to see the priestly hermits "seated on deer-skins spread under the shadow of Sala trees and engaged in teaching their students the Vedas, Sastras and other useful arts, as required by the latter."[128] They seem to have been given to a life of much self-denial and penance and sacrifices. Whether they lived as householders in villages and towns, or as hermits and ascetics in forests, their life seems to have been as simple as their learning high. Though, as hermits and ascetics in hermitages, they seem to have lived sometimes on the flesh of wild animals, or on wild rice gleaned and collected by themselves from fields or on fruits and roots gathered from the forests, and other times on the bounty of kings and wealthy men,[129] the householders in villages and towns seem to have engaged themselves in various kinds of occupations, agriculture, cattle rearing, medicine, corn-grinding and even gambling.[130]

This highly learned, though pious, priestly oligarchy or aristocracy, independent of the king and exempt from the ordinary exercise of the royal power, is not a peculiar feature of the Indian Aryans alone. It appears to have been a common characteristic of the Aryan race as a whole, whatever might be the country it had occupied, Greece, Rome or India. The ancient Greeks and Romans are

---

[127] Vishnupurana, IV. 3.

[128] Devi Bhagavata, V. 32, 26-27.

[129] Baudhayana, III. 2 and 3.

[130] Rig. IX. 112.

said to have had a similar kind of priestly oligarchy among them. In his City State of the Greeks and Romans (pp. 115-119, Ed. 1907) Fowler says as follows :—

"In the age of kingship, as we saw, the functions of government were religious, judicial and military. These functions have now passed out of the hands of the king and belong to the magistrate and councils of the artistocracy. Let us see how they might be used so as to favour the interests of the few as against those of the many. The secrets of the religion consisted of a knowledge of the ritual proper to each occasion ; the knowledge, that is, of the art of keeping the human inhabitants of the city on good terms with its divine members. Every public act was accompanied by a sacrifice, and all sacrifices must be performed in exactly the right way. The sacrificial hymns must be rightly sung ; the omens must be taken, the purificatory processions conducted exactly in the received manner, or the gods would not answer and bless. The whole life and happiness of the State depended on the proper performance of these necessary duties. Now in a State made up, as we have seen, by the union of lesser communities, each of which had its own peculiar worship conducted by its own noble family or families, it is plain that all these worships, now embodied in the State, must have remained in the hands of the aristocracy. The whole organisation of the State's religious life was theirs also. The regulation of festivals, of marriage, of funerals, of holy places and land belonging to the gods,—all that the Romans understood by the words *jus sacrum*,—was theirs and theirs only. For a person to meddle with such things, who was not qualified by birth or education or tradition nor expressly invited by the State as a reformer, was not only to interfere with the rights of a class, but positively to disturb the good relations of the City with its gods, and thus imperil its very life. Of these relations, and of this life the noble families were in a way trustees; what wonder then, if their trusteeship increased their pride and narrowed their sympathies, raising in them a growing contempt for men who know nothing of the will or the needs of the divine inhabitants of the City?

"So it was also in the religion of profane law, as it slowly disentangled itself from the law of religious usage. Here, too, the rule held good that all solemn acts must be performed according to prescribed order, if they were to have any binding force. Rules governing the tenure of land, rules governing the transference of all property by succession or sale, rules governing the treatment of evil-doers and the adjustment of all disputes, so far as they were administered by aristocracy only, they were as much matter of technical and traditional knowledge as the religious law and could not be administered save by those to whom a divine order had entrusted that knowledge. The executive of the State, in fact, was in the hands of the only true Statemen (Politai). What wonder, then, once more, if these men and their families believed themselves to be the only lawful possessors of secret of Government, as well as religion, which they might turn to their own particular advantage?

'Even in military matters—the third department of Government—the same tendency is seen; for the aristocracy took the greater risk in actual warfare, and were at greater expense than the commons in providing themselves with horses and superior arms. They, like the chivalry of the Middle Ages, were the flower of the State's Army; they had a greater stake in the State and they like their mediæval counterparts, came to look down on the people as beings who could not or would not fight, unworthy alike of honour on the battlefield and of power in the constitution.'

Thus we may be sure that in course of time there came to be a greater distinctness of outline of the position of the class to whom all the secrets and advantages belonged. While the State was not yet fully realised, while its elements were still in solution, this distinctness was less strong. But when the various elements of population came to face each other in the well-knit State, the idea of privilege began to make itself felt. The holders of the secrets which we have been describing, so soon as they began to use them for their advantage as a class, would cease to be thought of as heaven-appointed trustees, and would come to be considered as privileged." (The City State of the Greeks and the Romans, pp. 115-119. Ed. 1907.)

The same fact is briefly expressed by Mr. A.H.J. Grundige in his "Handbook of Greek Constitutional History" (p. 21, Ed. 1911).

"We may now form some idea of the power of this nobility of birth. In most cases its members had won their territory by the right of conquest, and were the large land-owners in the States. Their special claims to honour were the exclusive knowledge of its laws, and the sole possession of that citizenship which resulted from higher birth and from inherited wealth and culture. This was the rule of the best aristoi; and for a time these governments have been the truest aristocracies that the Greek would ever see. It was not merely the position, it was still more the qualities which made these men at once priest, judges, and soldiers that seemed unattainable by the common herd. Their ruler had a divine sanction; but the theocratic element was not oppressively present; it was less obvious than at Rome, for the clan worship, exclusive as it was, was less baneful than the inscrutable knowledge of the priestly colleges of the Roman Patriciate, which created a strong tie of interest between all the families of the privileged class, and professed to give rules for all things human and divine."

Having thus surveyed the physical and intellectual superiority which enabled the kings and the priestly class to put forward claims for special privileges and prerogatives fitting their positions, we may now turn our attention to the consideration of the peculiar nature of the privileges themselves :—

As a defender of the kingdom, the king seems to have been allowed the right of 'eating the rich'[131] by levying taxes and tributes from them[132] and of distributing treasures collected from taxation and plunder amongst his people, especially the priestly class in his own discretion. He had the right of passing judgments in civil and criminal cases, perhaps as decided in the people's assembly.[133] His was the right of bestowing handsome gifts on priests in sacrifices and in festivities. He seems to have been allowed the right of selecting his own priest from the family of the royal priest and of appointing the seven Ratnins or officers, such as the Commander of the army (Senapati), the charioteer (Suta), the village-headman (Gramani), the chamberlain (kshattar), the Collector of taxes (Sangrahitar), the distributor or divider of food (Bhagadugha) and the dice-player (akshvapa).[134]

He seems to have had his own private lands and cattle, as Sugrieva and other ancient kings had their Madhuvana or pleasure gardens. According to Ramayana, honey and fruits in the Madhuvana of Sugrieva became the spoils of the exulting monkey troops on their return from Lanka in the joy of having found out Sita in the Asoka

---

[131] Rig. I. 65, 4.

[132] A. V. XIX. 2, 6, and Rig. 173, 6.

[133] A. V. XIX. 24, 3.

[134] Tai. Samhita, I. 8, 9.

garden of Ravana. Even the queens and princes are said to have possessed their own lands and wealth in the Arthasastra (II. 7). Whether the Vedic kings had their private lands or not, depends on the view we take of their origin. If they were elected from among the common people or from among the Kshatriya class evolved out of the people themselves, it would follow that the elected kings continued in the enjoyment of the landed property which they must have had before election. If they were elected from the very beginning from among the descendants of the institution of the queens, it would follow that they had no private property of their own, the queens being allowed to have all the property as their own as in Travancore and Cochin.

As the resources of entering into a war or an agreement of peace lay with the kings, the question of war or peace seems to have rested with them alone. It cannot however be denied that he had to consult his own priests and officers and the people's assembly as well. Even in the matter of anointing their own eldest sons in the kingdom when they themselves grew old, ancient kings appear to have ascertained the view or inclination of their people's assembly. Dasaratha's attempt to gauze the opinion of his people and the assembly on the question of installing Rama on his throne is an instance on the point. Duryodhana's maltreatment of the Pandavas and their wife Draupudi against the verdict of his assembly seems to be an exception.

The king was called Vispati, lord of the people, as contrasted with the Brahmans. As Vispati, he had no royal power over the priests.

The levy of benevolences and special taxes and tolls, as stated in the Arthasastra, was a royal privilege of later period.

The king was a man among men: neither does he seem to have made, nor the people to have acquiesced in, his claim for divine birth or right, which, as will be seen later on, is a political expedient devised by politicians of the post-Kautilya period.

In addition to their prerogative of being independent of the king, the priest seems to have claimed and secured immunities in important judicial matters, as set forth in the following passages of the Yajurveda :—

"If a Brahman and a non-Brahman have a litigation, one (the king) should support the Brahman; if one supports the Brahman, one supports oneself; if one opposes the Brahman, one opposes oneself; therefore one should not oppose a Brahman (Tai. Samhita, II. 5, 12).

"Him who reviles a Brahman, he (the king) shall fine with a hundred; him who strikes a Brahman, he shall fine with a thousand; he who draws blood from him shall not behold the world of the Pitris." (Tai. Samhita, II. 6, 11).

The fines levied from the offender were paid not to the king, but to the Brahman, as a kind of Wergeld. The last sentence seems to mean that no funeral rites should be performed in the name of a slayer of a Brahman on his death.

In still clearer terms are enumerated the immunities of the priests in the Sutra literature. The Apastamba Sutra, for example, says as follows :—

"In his realm no Brahman should suffer hunger, sickness, cold, or heat, be it through want or intentionally." (Apa. II. 10, 25, 11.)

"The king who, without detriment to his servants, gives land and money to Brahmans according to their deserts gains endless worlds.

"They say that a king who is slain in attempting to recover the property of Brahmans performs a sacrifice where his body takes the place of the sacrificial post and at which an unlimited fee is given.

"A learned Brahman is free from taxes." (Apa. II, 10, 26, 1, 2, 10.)

Thus it is clear that the Vedic political constitution consisted of (1) a priestly aristocracy independent of the king and exempt from punishment for offences and from taxes and tolls on land and other property, and with acknowledged claims to protection from hunger, sickness, cold, or heat; (2) a king, elected at first and hereditary later; and (3) a state-assembly consisting of priests, nobles and the common people with powers to elect and banish kings, to restore banished kings, and to have an authoritative voice on all political and judicial matters of the state. The most troublesome element of the constitution was the priestly aristocracy with which the kings were, as already pointed out, at war for the sake of the mysterious cow, and perhaps on account of their exorbitant privileges also.[135]

---

[135] Vishnu Purana, 1, 13. Vena *versus* the Brahmans. How thi discord ended will be seen later on.

LECTURE VI.

THE EFFECT OF JAINISM AND BUDDHISM ON THE POLITICAL CONDITION OF INDIA.

At no time in the history of India had its priestly aristocracy a more desperate struggle for existence than during the Sutra period. Apart from splits in itself due to difference of opinion on matters of minute details in sacrifices, its dispute with the kings regarding the question of its privileges does not seem to have come to an end, though it had to set aside the question of cows on the defeat of Parasurama, its champion, and his flight to the West Coast corner of Southern India. The question of allowing the priests to continue in the enjoyment of their exhorbitant privileges seems to have been still under dispute. King Vena, for example, is said to have caused it to be everywhere proclaimed that no worship should be performed, no oblations offered and no gifts bestowed upon the Brahmans.[136]

What was worse still, there arose two successive separatist movements, one after another, with the set purpose of reforming and purifying the social and religious order of the Indian Aryan community as a whole. They were the movements founded by ruling princes after mature deliberation. The earlier of these two movements is known as Jainism, called after the name of Rishabha or Jina, the first founder and teacher of that religion. Of the 24 Tîrthankaras or teachers beginning with Rishabha

---

[136] Vishnu Purana, I. 13.

and ending with Vardhamâna Mahâvîra, all of whom seem to have belonged to the Kshatriya class or to ruling princes, the last three, Nemi or Arishtanemi, Parsvanâtha and Mahâvîra, seem to have been the most powerful preachers. Arishtanemi is stated to have been a prince and cousin of Krishna of the Yâdava race. The story, as narrated in the commentary of the Uttarâdhyayana Sûtra[137] says that when he was told that the herd of animals which he met in his procession preparatory to his marriage with Râjîmatî was being led to be slaughtered for the purpose of a banquet to be given in honour of his marriage and coronation in the Yâdava Kingdom, he relinquished his marriage and the kingdom in disgust and took to forest life following the orders of the old Tîrthankaras, and leaving the kingdom to his cousin Krishna. Parsvanatha who succeeded Arishtenemi, 773 B. C., as a Tîrthankara was a prince like his predecessor and was succeeded by Mahâvîra, a king like himself.

The object with which these Tîrthankaras embraced asceticism was not merely to emancipate themselves from the unending chain of birth and death, but to save the Aryan people from the social, religious and political bondage from which they believed them to be suffering. While they kept themselves under a stern religious discipline with a firm mind to conquer the six enemies, desire, anger, niggardliness, delusion, intemperance, and jealousy, and to attain emancipation by meditation and contemplation on the self or soul, they seem to have been preaching to the people at large to give up the social and religious customs of the Brâhmans and to practise as far as possible the observance of the four gifts,—the gift of food, gift of

[137] Jaina Series, published by Rao Bahadur Raja Dhanapalasimha, Vol. XLI, pp. 655-670.

protection of animal life, gift of medicine, and gift of true knowledge (Ahârbâhayabhaishajya sâstradâna[138]), as stated in the inscriptions of Hoisala Ballaladeva. While the first three gifts determine the guiding principle of the various activities which man may take upon himself as a social and industrial being, the last inculcates the necessity of his learning and teaching true knowledge, as taught in the philosophy of the Jainas. This philosophy is based partly upon the Upanishads and partly upon the atheistic philosophy of Kapila. The philosophy as expounded by Kapila, teaches us that there are only two principal entities, man and nature, man suffering or enjoying according to the attitude of his mind under his control, and Nature having a productive power manifesting or presenting to man the externally indestructible matter in its various forms. Attachment to Nature brings pain to man, while non-attachment or neutrality by merging self in self brings on emancipation to him. Accordingly Sankhya philosophy knows neither God nor Dharma, charity or virtue in any form. The Jaina philosophy, though equally atheistic, is an improvement on the Sankhya by the addition of Dharma[139] as a means for the attainment of emancipation.[140] Hence knowing neither God nor an authoritative revealed text, Jainism has rejected the Vedas of the Brâhmans with all its animal sacrifices, as inconsistent with the promise of abstaining from injury and cruelty to animal life.[141] Apart from the four gifts and from rendering service to saints, teachers, ascetics, the infirm, the ganas, kulas, Sanghas, the good, and the enlightened, as inculcated in the

---

[138] Inscription in Banasankari temple at Udri in Sorab, Shimoga District, Mysore.

[139] Uttaradhyâyana sutra, p. 577, verse 20.

[140] Tatvarthasutra, I. 1, 2, 3 & X. 1.

[141] Gift No. 2 quoted above.

Tatvârthasutra (IX. 24), there is no other Dharma which a Jaina has to know. The Jainas do not seem tired of discussing the question of Dharma and Adharma from various points of view. A religious practice, a social custom or a political duty or function is according to the Jainas a Dharma or virtuous practice only when it is not antagonistic with the four gifts enumerated above. Accordingly the Vedas are no revealed texts, as they teach sacrifices inconsistent with Abhayadâna or promise of protection. Nor are they eternal, as believed by the Brahmans, since no human utterance or writing can possibly be eternal.[142]

Neither during the Vedic period nor during the Jaina and the Buddhist periods till the first few centuries of the Christian era was there such a rigid caste system as prevailed later. The people were divided into classes with rights of connubium and commensality with each other. When the Jainas had formed an order of their own, they had observed the same class system without any detriment to their faith and practice.[143] Along with such antecaste customs as flesh-eating, plurality of wives married from other classes inclusive of the Sudras, interdining with Sudras and the like, the Brahmans seem to have been imposing on suspected persons some restrictions to the right of connubium and commensality and to the right of social intercourse with the Chandalas. Restriction to the right of connubium and commensality is thus referred to in the Taittirîya Samhita (VI. 2, 6).

"On a place of sacrifice which is distinctly marked should he cause him to sacrifice regarding the person, of whom they have doubts as to admitting him to common meals or to marriage."

---

[142] Nandi Sutra, pp. 20-30.

[143] Uttaradhyâyana sutra, p. 156.

The Jainas seem to have condemned these and other exclusive and indiscreet or intemperate customs as inconsistent with Dharma or Virtue. As to the question of untouchability of the outcastes, the Jainas have condemned it outright as a mere profession incapable of being translated into practice, inasmuch as the wind is found to carry minute particles of strong-smelling flowers and fruits in the hands of the outcastes right through the nose into the very stomach of the Brahman.[144]

Amitagati, a Jaina-writer, who, as stated by himself in the introduction to his work, Dharmapariksha, lived in 1014 A. D. makes a Gandharva, an imaginary character, talk of the widow marriage and other customs of the Brahmans in a condemnatory tone, as follows :—

"When I saw my widowed mother being wedded to another, I narrated my relationship with her and asked the pious men, 'pray tell me whether there is no sin in her being married to another.'

"When it is said that Draupadi had the five sons of Pandu as her husbands, where is sin for thy mother, if she has two husbands. The husband being dead by misfortune, the maiden, though once betrothed, deserves the right of marriage consecration for a second time. The woman that has brought forth a child has to wait eight years, while a maiden should wait only four years before marrying another, if the husband has gone abroad. If second husbands are married for reasons mentioned in the five enumerated cases, there is no guilt for women, as stated by Vyasa and others."

By way of condemning the customs of the Brahmans and of pointing out the nature of a true Brahman, a true Kshatriya, a true Vaisya, and a true Sudra, Jayaghosha, a

---

[144] Nandi Sutra, pp. 344-6, Calcutta Ed.

Jaina ascetic, is stated to have instructed a Brahman named Vijayaghosha in the following passages of the Uttarâdhyâyana Sutra (XXV. 24, 33) :—

" He who does not injure living beings in any of the three ways (thoughts, words, and actions), him we call a Brahmana. He who does not speak untruth from anger or for fun, from greed or from fear, him we call a Brahmana.

By one's actions one becomes a Brahmana, or a Kshatriya or a Vaisya or a Sudra."

In the dialogue between Nami and Indra who advised him to retain royalty instead of renouncing it, the duties of a king according to the reformed notions of the Jainas are thus hinted[145] :—

In reply to Indra's advice to Nami to erect a wall, gates, and battlements, to dig a moat and to construct Sataghnis, he answers that faith is his fortress, penance and self-control the bolt of its gate, patience its strong wall, zeal his bow, and carefulness in walking its string.

In reply to his advice to punish thieves, robbers and burglars, Nami answers that men frequently apply punishment wrongly, by putting the innocent in prison and by setting the true criminal at liberty.

In reply to Indra's advice to him to conquer his foes, to perform sacrifices and to feed Brahmans, Nami answers that though a man should conquer thousands of valiant foes, greater will be his victory if he conquers nobody but himself ; that one should fight with one's own self and conquer the five senses and anger, pride, delusion and greed ; and that self-control is better than sacrifices and gifts to Brahmans.

---

[145] Uttaradhyâyana, IX. 22-39.

Still stronger was the denunciation hurled by the Buddhists on the Brahmans. In the Tevigga Sutta, a dialogue between a Brahman named Vasettha and Gotama on the character of the Brahmans, the defects of the Brahmans, are thus pointed out.

Gotama asks Vasettha :—

"Now what think you, Vasettha, are the Brahmans versed in the Vedas in the possession of wives and wealth, or are they not ?"

Vasettha replied :—

"They are, Gotama."

"Have they anger in their hearts, or have they not ?"

"They have, Gotama."

"Do they bear malice, or do they not ?"

"They do, Gotama."

"Are they pure in heart, or are they not ?"

"They are not, Gotama."

"Have they self-mastery, or have they not ?"

"They have not, Gotama."

"Very good Vasettha. That these Brahmans versed in the Vedas and yet bearing anger and malice in their hearts, sinful, and uncontrolled, should after death, when the body is dissolved, become united to Brahma, who is free from anger and malice, sinless and has self-mastery—such a condition of things has no existence."[146]

The sacred and secular learning of the Brahmans and their capacity to perform various sacrifices to secure good, or to avert bad results either to the king or to the people are thus denounced in the Tevigga Sutta (II. 3) :—

"Or whereas some Samana Brahmans, who live on the food provided by the faithful, continue to gain a livelihood by such low arts and such lying practices as these,

[146] Uttaradhyâyana, I. 38.

that is to say, by foretelling future events, as these : 'There will be a sortie by the king.' 'There will not be a sortie by the king.' 'The king within the city will attack.' 'The king outside the city will retreat.' 'The king within the city will gain victory.' 'The king outside the city will be defeated.' 'The king outside the city will be the conquerer.' Thus prophesying to this one victory, to that one defeat."

" This is the kind of goodness that he has. "

" Likewise by predicting that there will be abundant rainfall, abundant harvest, famine, disturbances, sickness or health ; or by drawing deeds, making up accounts, giving pills, making verses, or arguing points of casuistry, or by giving advice touching the taking in marriage, or the giving in marriage, the forming of alliances, or dissolution of connections ; by teaching spells to procure prosperity, or to cause adversity to others ; or by worshipping the sun, or by worshipping Brahma, by spitting fire out of their mouths'—this, too, is the kind of goodnes that he has."[147]

While under this severe criticism directed by the Jainas and the Buddhists against the social, religious and political views of the Brahman oligarchy, the firm hold which it had on the peoples' mind was fast loosening, the constructive organisation made by the separatists to reform the Aryan Society in all its aspects appeared to render that old oligarchy quite powerless to survive. Though atheistic, it was a humanitarian religion based upon justice, charity, and brotherhood. As every man was obliged to free himself at all costs from the six inimical passions, desire, anger, greed, delusion, lust and jealousy, he had no cause whatever to apprehend injustice

[147] *Ibid*, II.5,6.

from his fellow beings. Men and women were required to regard each other as brothers and sisters and to be kind not only to their fellow beings, but also to beasts. The duty of kings and rich householders was according to the new gospel to construct alms-houses, to erect hospitals both for men and beasts, to plant avenue trees, to open roads and to dig wells of water at intervals here and there. It was the duty of the Sangha, the Buddhist order of monks, to preach to the people at large and prevail upon them to free themselves from all passions and to tread on the new path of Dharma, justice and charity, declaring *abhaya* or promise of protection from fear to all. It was a league of men with sincere and open heart, but not of nations with lip sympathy and cunning heart. Under the protection of this kingdom of virtue or natural law (Dhammachakka) there was no room for criminals, robbers, or enemies. Kings might disband their huge army and spend their revenue in relieving the misery of the needy and the infirm. There could be no talk of war, for who would dare to raise his weapons against a league of men devoted to the service of Natural justice and dharma ? It may be presumed without any fear of contradiction that among the several Aryan and non-Aryan kingdoms from the Himalayas down to the Cape Comorin, there was no kingdom that was deaf to the preachings of the Jainas and the Buddhists. Jaina and Buddhist monasteries began to rise in numbers in all the kingdoms throughout the length and breadth of India, as confirmed by a number of Jaina and Buddhist inscriptions already discovered and still under discovery. Benares, North West Provinces, Rajaputana, Central India, Gujerat, the Pandya and Chola kingdom, and Mysore,—all teemed with Jaina and Buddhist settlements and monasteries.

To allay all fear of exaggeration at rest and to confirm the assertions I have ventured to make here, some of the edicts of Asoka, the first Indian Emperor, are quoted below :—

" Here in the Capital no animal may be slaughtered for sacrifice, nor may holiday feasts be held, for His Majesty King Priyadarsin sees manifold evil in holiday feasts."

Edict I.

" Everywhere in dominions of His Majesty King Priyadarsin, and likewise in the neighbouring realms such as those of the Chola, Pandya, Satiyaputra and Keralaputra, in Ceylon, in the dominions of the Greek King Antiochus, and in those of the other kings subordinate to that Antiochus—everywhere, on behalf of His Majesty have two kinds of remedies been disseminated, remedies for men and remedies for beasts......on the roads trees have been planted and wells have been dug for the use of man and beast."

Edict II.

" Obedience to father and mother is good ; liberality to friends, acquaintances, relatives, Brahmans, and ascetics is good ; avoidance of extravagance and violence of language is good. The clergy will thus instruct the lieges in detail."

Edict III.

" Now, by reason of the practice of piety, instead of the war-drum, the sound of the drum of piety is heard."

Edict IV.

" Even for a person to whom lavish liberality is impossible, the virtues of mastery over the senses, purity of mind, gratitude and fidelity are always meritorious."

Edict XXI.

Of all the Edicts of Asoka, the most important is the thirteenth Edict entitled the 'True Conquest.' It is the edict in which the Emperor has proclaimed to the world at large his full belief in the efficiency of the Buddhist law of piety as a real force in making a true conquest of man, not by weapons but by appealing to his moral sense and conscience and by pointing out the ruin which he may bring upon himself and others by addictions to passions. It runs as follows:—

"His Majesty King Priyadarsin in the ninth year of his reign conquered the Kalingas.[148] One hundred and fifty thousand persons were thence carried away captive, one hundred thousand were there slain, and many times that number perished.

"Ever since the annexation[149] of the Kalingas, His Majesty has zealously protected the Law of Piety, has been devoted to that law, and has proclaimed its precepts.

"His Majesty feels remorse on account of the conquest of the Kalingas, because, during the subjugation of a previously unconquered country, slaughter, death, and taking away captive, of the people necessarily occur, whereat His Majesty feels profound sorrow and regret.

"There is, however, another reason for His Majesty feeling still more regret, inasmuch as in such a country dwell Brahmans and ascetics, men of different sects, and householders who all practice obedience to elders, obedience

---

[148] The Kalingas, Kalimgani; the country extending along the coast of Bay of Bengal from the Mahanadi river on the north to or beyond the Krishna river on the south; often called 'the Three Kalingas,' which are supposed to be the kingdoms of Amaravati. In this edict the name is used in both the singular and the plural. The Dhauli and Jaugada rock inscriptions are situated in this conquered province.

[149] Conquered, vijita; 'annexed,' ladheshu.

to father and mother, obedience to teachers, proper treatment of friends, acquaintances, comrades, relatives, slaves and servants, with fidelity of devotion.[150] To such people dwelling in that country happen violence, slaughter, and separation from those whom they love.

"Even those persons who are themselves protected retain the affections undiminished:—ruin falls on their friends, acquaintances, comrades, and relatives, and in this way violence is done to those who are personally unhurt.[151] All this diffused misery[152] is matter of regret to His Majesty. For there is no country where such communities are not found including others besides Brahmans and ascetics, nor is there any place in any country where the people are not attached to some one sect or other.[153]

"The loss of even the hundredth or the thousandth part of the persons who were then slain, carried away captive, or done to death in Kalinga would now be a matter of deepregret to His Majesty.

"Although a man should do him an injury, His Majesty holds that it must be patiently borne, so far as it can possibly be borne.

"Even upon the forest tribes in his dominions His Majesty has compassion, and he seeks their conversion, inasmuch as the might even of His Majesty is based on repentance. They are warned to this effect—'Shun

---

[150] That is to say, who practise the dharma, or Law of Piety, of which a summary is given.

[151] That is to say, they are hurt in their feelings.

[152] 'Diffused misery,' equivalent to Bühler's 'all this falls severally on men.' M. Senart denies the distributive sense of pratibhagam, and translates (i. 309) '*toutes les violences de ce genre.*'

[153] This sentence is translated from the fuller form in the Kalsi text, as corrected by M. Senart from the newly discovered Girnar fragment, J. R. A. S, for 1900, p. 339.

evildoing, that ye may escape destruction'; because His Majesty desires for all animate beings security, control over the passions, peace of mind, and joyousness.[154]

"And this is the chiefest conquest, in His Majesty's opinion—the conquest of the Law of Piety; this also is that effected by His Majesty both in his own dominions and in all the neighbouring realms as far as six hundred leagues[155] even to where the Greek King named Antiochus dwells, and beyond that Antiochus to where dwell the four Kings severally named Ptolemy, Antigonus, Magus, and Alexander;[156] and in the south, the Kings of the Cholas, and Pandyas, and of Ceylon,[157] and likewise here, in the King's dominions, among the Yonas, and Kambojas, in Nabhaka of the Nabhitis, among the Bhojas and Pitinikas, among the Andhras and Pulindas,[158] everywhere men follow the Law of Piety as proclaimed by His Majesty.

---

154 "Joyousness" rabhasiye (Shahb), madvam (Girnar), madava (Kalsi). The translation of the first sentence of this paragraph is in accordance with M. Senart's corrections.

155 'League' yojana, a varying measure, commonly taken as equal to seven or eight miles.

156 Antiochus Theos, of Syria; Ptolemy Philadelphus, of Egypt; Antigonus Gonatas, of Macedonia; Alexander, of Epirus; Magas, of Cyrene.

157 The Chola capital was at Uraiyur near Trichinopoly; the Pandya capital was at Madura. Tishya (Tissa) was the contemporary King of Ceylon.

158 The Yonas (Yavanas) must mean the clans of foreign race (not necessarily Greek) on the north-western frontier, included in the Empire; the Kambojas seem to have been also a north-western tribe.

I cannot offer any explanation of 'Nabhaka of the Nabhitis' (Bühler).

The Andhras inhabited the country near the Krishna river, at the southern extremity of the Kalingas. Subsequently, they established a powerful kingdom. The Pulindas seem to have occupied the central parts of the Peninsula. The Pitinikas may have been the inhabitants of Paithana on the Godaveri. (See M. Senart in Ind. Ant., XX, 348, and

"Even in those regions where the envoys of His Majesty do not penetrate,[159] men now practise and will continue to practise the Law of Piety as soon as they hear the pious proclamation of His Majesty issued in accordance with the Law of Piety.

"And the conquest which has thereby been everywhere effected, causes a feeling of delight.

"Delight is found in the conquests made by the Law.[160] Nevertheless, that delight is only a small matter. His Majesty thinks nothing of much importance save what concerns the next world.

"And for this purpose has this pious edict been written, to wit, that my sons and grandsons, as many as they may be, may not suppose it to be theirs to effect a new conquest; and that even when engaged in conquest by arms they may find pleasure in patience and gentleness, and may regard as the only true conquest that which is effected through the Law of Piety,[161] which avails both for this world and the next. Let all their pleasure be the pleasure in exertion, which avails both for this world and the next."

Thus the kingdom of Righteousness which began with Buddha with its eightfold noble path of right views, right aspirations, right speech, right conduct, right livelihood, right effort, right mindfulness, and right contemplation, took a firm stand in the land during the righteous imperial rule of Asoka, muzzling for years to come the

J.R.A.S. for 1900, p. 340). The names enumerated are those of border tribes under the suzerainty of Asoka.

[159] Missionaries were dispatched in the eleventh or twelfth year of the reign.

[160] Bühler's rendering accidentally omits the words Ladha (bhoti) priti dhrama vijayaspi).

[161] I think I have given the meaning correctly, and in accordance with the intention of Bühler.

Brahman oligarchy, its Vedic Gods and animal sacrifices. It must be admitted to the credit of India and her law-abiding sons that this stupendous change in her social, religious, and political institutions was so quietly and peacefully effected with no trace of bloodshed that even to the irritated Brahman oligarchy it appeared as an illusory phenomena brought about by the magic wand of a skilful wizard. "This son of Suddhodana," says the Agnipurana (Chapter 16, 3), "was the greatest deluder. He deluded the Daityas and led them away from the Vedic Dharma." Compared with persecutions and martyrdoms which attended the spread of Christianity and its various stages of its reform and the reign of terror which preceded and followed political reforms brought about under the influence of Christianity in Europe[162] the quiet and peaceful rise and fall of Jainism and Buddhism in India purely in virtue of its intrinsic vitality and decrepitude appears to be a romantic tale, the like of which the world has never seen. Whether this is due to the peculiar soil and climate of India or to the inexplicable temperament of her people is a question which history has yet to solve.[163]

---

[162] Early Church History by J. V. Bartl.

[163] The travels of the Chinese Pilgrim Yuan Chwang, Vols. I and II.

LECTURE VII.

THE EMPIRE-BUILDING POLICY OF THE POLITICIANS OF THE KAUTILYA PERIOD.

In the kingdom of righteousness (Dhammachakka) firmly set up by the Buddhists in India there was no distinction between man and man, king or priest, monk or householder, trader or tiller of the soil; all were on the same level. In common with others, each had his clearly defined duty before him, the duty of conquering the six inimical passions and of preparing himself for his final Nirvana or emancipation from the bondage of transmigration. Except his own exertion, he had no need to seek other means, of which there was none at all. He needed neither a god nor a priest to help him in his attempt to relieve himself. He was his own god or Satan according as he walked on the righteous or unrighteous path. If he were born a king, all that he had to do was to direct his officers to superintend the works of Dhamma and insist on every one's duty of observing the Law of Piety, toleration, and charity. None had need to perform mystic sacrifices for securing mystic aims. As all had to tread on the same path of Dhamma, there could be no enemies and consequently no war, necessitating the employment of a huge army. If he were a rich trader, he might continue his profession and accumulate wealth not for his own selfish purposes and ultimate destruction, but for the meritorious purpose of charity to the needy. If he were a priest, he could very well understand his own duty to himself or better than others, inasmuch as he had a cultured mind to aid him in his attempt to reach the final goal.

He had no need for any texts or prayer, revealed or unrevealed, either for his own use or for the use of others. The only qualification which man needed was the knowledge of correct view, correct conduct, correct thought, correct mode of obtaining a livelihood, correct speech, correct meditation, and correct tranquillity.[164] If one succeeded in attaining that knowledge, it would be for one's own good. One had no need to impose upon others and claim privileges therefor.

In this kingdom of Righteousness, there was room neither for a crafty high priest nor for an honest high priest, neither for the sacred Vedas nor for the animal sacrifices enjoined by the Vedas. The Brahman oligarchy which had so much to do in the old social, religious, and political order of the Aryans had to come down from its old high pedestal and relinquishing its claims to exclusive privileges, merge itself among the people with no distinction whatever. At the most he could be a monk, if he could boast of a cultured mind. His Vedas and sacrifices forget he must. It is more than probable that owing to the conversion to Jainism and Buddhism of a number of learned Brahmans that knew the traditional interpretation of the Vedas and of Vedic sacrifices, the true Vedic learning was lost and that mere Vedic recitation remained with the illiterate minority or majority that still obstinately adhered to its old faith. Perhaps it was a majority of Brahmans that stood aloof looking with mortification at the wonderful spread of Jainism and Buddhism at the expense of Brahminism in the land, since it is from those irreconcilables that modern Brahmans have sprung up and revived their old Vedic lore.

---

[164] Buddhist Suttas: Foundation of the kingdom of Righteousness, pp. 144-147.

Now that Jainism and Buddhism were spreading in the land like wild fire with no such devastation as wild fire commonly does and with no malice, hatred or injury to any one, what could the helpless Brahman do? None needed him as before, yet none injured him apparently. He had no real grievance against any, but his own destiny. The kings and the people whom he had under his clutches left him to his destiny now. Hopeless and desperate as was the task which the Brahman had to undertake in order to regain his lost supremacy in the land, he seems to have entertained no doubts as to the means which he had to employ to succeed in this attempt. Under similar circumstances the Western Brahman or trained politicians would have surely appealed to arms, as he had more often than once done in all his revolutionary propaganda, whether social, religious or political. Time is precious with the Western. He would not wait and spend time in thinking of any peaceful means for success in his attempt. Brute force has a charm for him and he employs it for good or bad. But the Eastern Brahman differs from him in this. He is not for arms where he believes that skill can crown him with success. Though the Eastern has shown his dogged determination in fighting as obstinately as the Western in the battlefield, still it is certainly a mistake to suppose that he prefers the sword to all other means as much as the Western does. Even Professor Wilson, the translator of the Vishnu Purana and other Sanskrit works could not shake himself off from this characteristic bias or notion. While remarking on an ambiguous passage of the Vishnupurana about the conflict of the Brahmans and the Buddhists he seems to think that the Brahmans took to arms and extirpated the Jainas and the Buddhists whereas the truth is that the Brahmans overcame the Buddhists rather by employing peaceful means than sword.

The passage of the Vishnupurana together with his remark runs as follows :—

" The delusions of the false teacher paused not with the conversion of the Daityas to the Jaina and Buddha heresies; but with various erroneous tenets he prevailed upon others to apostolize, until the whole were led astray, and deserted the doctrines and observances inculcated by the three Vedas. Some then spake evil of the sacred books; some blasphemed the gods; some treated sacrifices and other devotional ceremonies with scorn; and others calumniated the Brahmans. 'The precepts,' they cried, 'that lead to the injury of animal life (in sacrifices) are highly reprehensible. To say, that casting butter into flame is productive of reward, is mere childishness. If Indra, after having obtained godhead by multiplied rites is fed upon the wood used as fuel in holy fire he is lower than a brute which feeds at least upon leaves. If an animal slaughtered in religious worship is, thereby, raised to heaven, would it not be expedient for a man who institutes a sacrifice to kill his own father for a victim? If that which is eaten by one, at a Sraddha, gives satisfaction to another, it must be unnecessary for one who resides at a distance to bring food for presentation in person. First, then let it be determined what may be rationally believed by mankind; and then,' said their interpreceptor, 'you will find that felicity may be expected from my instructions. The words of authority, mighty Asuras, do not fall from heaven: the text that has reason is, alone, to be acknowledged by me and by such as you are.' By such and similar lessons the Daityas were perverted, so that not one of them admitted the authority of the Vedas. When the Daityas had thus declined from the path of the holy writings, the deities took courage and gathered together for battle. Hostilities, accordingly, were renewed; but the demons were none defeated and slain by the gods, who had adhered to the righteous path. The armour of religion which had formerly protected the Daityas had been discarded by them; and upon its own abandonment followed their destruction :—

(Vishnupurana, Book III, Chap. VIII.)

Commenting on the last few sentences of this passage, Professor Wilson remarks in the footnote as follows :—

"We may have, in this conflict of orthodox divinities and heretical Daityas, some correct allusion to political troubles growing out of religious differences, and the final predominance of Brahmanism. Such occurrences seem to have preceded the invasion of India by the Muhammadans and prepared the way for their victories."

The translator seems to think that though the war between the Buddhists and the Brahmans brought victory to the latter, it rendered India too weak to repel the disastrous attack by the Muhammadans. But I am inclined to believe that the success of the Brahmans was to a greater extent due to the employment of peaceful means than to open warfare, though there was, as will be seen later on, some war not however, between the Buddhist monks and the Brahman priests, but between Buddhist kings and aboriginal tribes incited by the Brahmans. The means employed by the Brahmans seem to have been threefold : social change, religious reformation, and political reorganisation, as needed by the times.

To free themselves from the Jaina and Buddhistic invectives upon their social customs, they had to give up some of their social customs such as plurality of wives, widow marriage, and Niyoga or the custom of deputing a stranger to beget a son on the wife of some one else. Though approved of by Gautama, Bodhayana, and other Sutra writers, these customs seem to have disappeared under the strong condemnation of the later Smriti writers by the first few centuries of the Christian era. Though plurality of wives had knit the Brahman and other three classes together and tended for the unification of all classes, still the Brahmans had been obliged to give it up and to isolate themselves into a caste by adopting endogamy. Likewise they had to give up flesh eating and by becoming vegetarians they discontinued interdining with non-vegetarians.

In the religious field they gave up most of their animal sacrifices, or performed very few of them on rare occasions. They now turned their attention to the study of the Upanishads and improved their philosophy so as to include all that the Jainas and the Buddhists had taught as their own. The one excellent and attractive feature which the Brahmanic philosophy had and which both Jainism and to some extent Buddhism entirely lacked was theism. The Jainas consider world to be eternal, *i.e.*, having neither a beginning nor a creator, but destined to end. They admit, however, the existence of a Brahma or Isvara, not as a creator, but merely as an ideal Being to be meditated upon. Nor is he considered as a Saviour. The Buddhists, on the other hand, are agnostics and neither admit nor deny the existence of a creator or saviour of the world. To refute this doctrine by pointing out its hollowness, the Brahmans had to take in the aid of their logic, as taught in the Nyaya and Vaiseshika schools just then founded for the very purpose. Side by side with these philosophic schools, there was Badarayana engaged in the stupendous task of interpreting the various Upanishads so as to mean a single central idea of Brahma, the transcendental Being and its various aspects. Jaimini had a similar mighty task of expounding Vedic exegetics, and Patanjali, the science of meditation or Rajayoga. Panini, Vararuchi and Patanjali had addressed themselves to the huge task of preparing an excellent Sanskrit Grammar, the like of which the world has never seen. It was for the purpose of having a pure learned language with no scope for such ungrammatical forms as "Korbhavan ? Sappoham," "Who are you ? I am a serpent." The error in this expression is that the letter 'r' which has to come before 'pa' in Sarpa was inserted, between 'o' and 'b' 'in Korbhavan.' In order to carry on their polemics against the Jainas and the Buddhists, the Brahmans s em to have required a refined language in contrast with the vulgar Pali language in which the separatists carried on their propaganda.

Likewise there arose at the same period a number of Smriti writers or codifiers of customs, such as Bhrigu, Yagnyavalkya, Parasara, Narada, and others who all endeavoured to the best of their ability to take stock of all ancient customs and record them, commending or condemning practices according as they appeared suitable or unsuitable to the spirit of their times, in the light of the reformed notions of the Jaina and Buddhist moralists.

Spurred on with the idea of representing Brahmanism in the most brilliant colours, there were also others who turned their attention to works on medicine and other useful arts. They were Agnivesa, Charaka, Susruta, Vatsyayana, Sudraka, and Kalidas, to mention only a few among them.

Theism or Atheism or Agnosticism ? was the question at issue between the Brahmans on the one hand and the Jainas and the Buddhists on the other. The syllogism which the Brahman logicians employed to defeat their opponents in dispute was, as set forth in their works on logic, of the following form :—

The world is the work of an intelligent designer : whatever is the work of an intelligent designer, like a piece of cloth or a pot has an agent to design. Therefore the world has an agent as its designer That designer is termed Brahma or Isvara or God or Creator It appears that as accomplished disputants, the Jainas and the Buddhists were as good as the Brahmans. Finding it hard to vanquish their opponents in dispute, the Brahmans seem to have consoled themselves by giving expression to the lame though significant threat, as set forth in the proverbial saying that if there be no Creator, there would be no harm to the theist; but if there be one, the atheist would be doomed.

Having thus vindicated themselves on the questions affecting their social and religious views, the Brahmans seem to have girded their loins to take advantage of the changed political conditions of the times. In addition to the three old famous political schools of Manu, Sukra, and Brihaspati, no fewer than a dozen new political schools, such as that of Parasara, Bharadvaja, Kaunapadanta, Vatavyadhi, Visalaksha, Pisuna, Pisuna-putra, Bahudanti-putra, Kautilya, Katyayana, Kinjalka, Ghotamukha and Charayana seem to have buried themselves in propounding political theories, some in favour of Kshatriya monarchy, Bharadvaja in favour of Brahman monarchy,[165] and Kautilya[166] holding both monarchical and republican forms of government equally good, all however being disposed to shape their views in the interests of Brahmanism.[167] All these thinkers seem to have been unanimous in advocating skilful intrigue as a means preferable to war to achieve an end. Kautilya says :—" The arrow shot by an archer may or may not kill a single man ; but skilful intrigue devised by wise men can kill even those who are in the womb."[168]

---

[165] Arthasastra, V. 6.

[166] *Ibid*, I. 17.

[167] *Ibid*, I. 3.

[168] Artha., X. 6, & also compare XIII. 4, etc.

Accordingly the means advocated by Kautilya to successfully carry out an intrigue is conciliation, bribery, and sowing the seeds of dissension.[169] Only when these means fail, war is advocated as the last means to achieve an end. In advocating the battle of intrigue as a better means than open warfare neither Kautilya nor his contemporary politicians seem to have troubled themselves with the moral aspect of the question. According to them the end that is sought for is all in all. As to the means, it may be fair or foul, moral or immoral. The business of a politician is to learn the art of intrigue and seek the favour of a king who is endowed with amiable qualities and possessed of all the elements of sovereign power, such as regal qualities, a good minister, a fertile territory, strong forts, sound finance, a powerful army and a trustworthy ally.[170] He has then to turn his attention to the preparation of a plan to conquer the king's enemies and make him an emperor. A king may be a friend or an enemy according to the territory he occupies with reference to that of the conqueror. Whoever is situated immediately on the circumference of the conqueror's territory is his enemy. One next to the enemy is his friend. Then comes the enemy's friend and then the conqueror's friend's friend and the enemy's friend's friend. Likewise in the rear of the conqueror there may be two enemies and two friends. Along with these there may be a neutral king and a mediator. Kautilya seems to have had in his mind the twelve zodiacal signs of the moon's or the sun's ecliptic in constituting a complete circle with the territories of the 12 kings, the conqueror, his five enemies, four friends, and two neutrals. That it is probably the zodiacal divisions that have suggested the idea

---

[169] *Ibid*, IX. 17.

[170] Artha, V. 4.

of the circle of twelve kings, is hinted in verse 81 of the second canto of the Sisupala Vadha. The verse translated into English runs as follows :—

"Just as the day-making Sun among the 12 suns is endowed with a prosperous career, so the conqueror who conceals no desire to conquer is endowed with a prosperous career among the 12 kings."

Politicians seem to have differed in their views regarding the question of determining the probable constituents of a circle of states that are likely to be at war with each other. The unit of a circle of states likely to be at war with each other according to Maya is said to consist of four kings, a conqueror, his enemy, his friend, and a neutral.[171] According to Puloma and Indra, the same is said to consist of two more kings, a rear-enemy and a mediator in addition to the four mentioned above.[172] In defining a unit of a circle of states as that which consists of three, four, six or twelve kings, the chief aim seems merely to point out the minimum or maximum number of kings to be subdued by the conqueror. That such is the aim, is confirmed by Kautilya's own statement in the Arthasastra. In XIII. 4, he says as follows :—

"Having seized the territory of his enemy close to his country, the conqueror should direct his attention to that of the Madhyama king; this being taken, he should catch hold of that of the neutral king. (1) This is the first way to conquer the world. In the absence of the Madhyama and neutral kings, he should, in virtue of his own excellent qualities, win the heart of his enemy's subjects and then direct his attention to other remote enemies. (2) This is the second way. In the absence

---

[171] Kamandaka, VIII. 2.

[172] *Ibid*, VIII. 21.

of a circle of states, he should conquer his friend or his enemy by hemming each between his own force and that of his enemy or that of his friend. (3) This is the third way Or he may put down an almost invincible immediate enemy. Having doubled his power by this victory, he may attack a second enemy; having trebled his power by this victory, he may attack a third. (4) This is the fourth way to conquer the world."

Thus in the view of Kautilya, friends or foes are merely relative terms depending on their positions either remote or immediate to the territory of the conqueror. So long as a king happens to be of help to the conqueror and with no territory adjacent to that of the conqueror, he is regarded as a friend. The moment he happens to own his territory close to that of the conqueror, he becomes an enemy to be conquered when the conqueror considers that his resources of men and money are enough to undertake the task According to Kautilya might, expediency, and self-aggrandisement are the chief objects for consideration and religion, morality and agreements of peace are of secondary or no consideration.[173] "Whoever," says Kautilya, "is rising in power may break the agreement of peace."[174]

The means employed to achieve the end in view is thus stated by Kautilya himself:

"Intrigue, spies, winning over the enemy's people, siege, and assault are the five means to capture a fort."[175]

How Kautilya succeeded in installing Chandragupta Maurya on the throne of the Nandas by employing the means mentioned above and paved the way for the mighty empire of Asoka, the grandson of Chandragupta, is a

[173] Artha., VII., 17.

[174] *Ibid.*

[175] Artha., XIII. 4.

historical fact known to all. It is intrigue carried on by skilful employment of spies trained in all sorts of professions that has enabled the politicians of the Kautilya period to succeed in their mighty task of building an empire favourable for the cause of Brahmanism. It is Buddhism itself that is answerable for their success and for its own downfall and ruin. Under the highly moral religion of the Jainas and the Buddhists, their kings became religiously and morally strong and politically too weak to withstand the attack of drunken fanatics and tumbled one after another like a pack of cards.

LECTURE VIII.

ESPIONAGE.

According to Kautilya and other politicians of his period espionage is one of the five means to build an empire by seizing villages after villages, cities after cities and forts after forts.[176] Though the credit of organizing an efficient system of espionage as a state machinery to carry out their imperial policy belongs to the politicians of the Kautilya period and especially to Kautilya, there is evidence to prove that it existed in some form or other even earlier than the times of Kautilya. "Spies are the eyes of kings" is a proverbial saying current among the people from time immemorial. Even during the Vedic period spies seem to have been largely employed not merely to ascertain validity or invalidity in the statements of parties and witnesses in criminal and civil cases tried by the king or the state assembly, but also to gather correct and reliable information as to the movements of tribal settlements of inimical tendency or disposition. The following passages from the Rigveda not only confirm this view but also indicate the class of people from whom spies were recruited and why :—

"Varuna, wearing golden mail, hath clad himself in a shining robe; His spies are seated round." I. 25, 13.

"Send thy spies forward, fleetest in thy motion; be never deceived, the guardian of this people. From him who, near or far, is bent on evil, and

---

[176] Artha., XIII. 4.

let no trouble sent from thee overcome us." IV. 4, 3.

"From the wide earth, O Varuna, and Mitra, from the great lofty heaven, ye, bounteous givers,

Have set in fields amid the plants your spies who visit every spot and watch unceasing." VII. 61, 8.

"Varuna's spies, sent forth upon their errand survey the two world halves well-formed and fashioned.

Wise are they, *holy, skilled in sacrifices, the furtherance of praise songs of the prudent.*" VII. 87, 3.

"They stand not still, they never close their eyelids, those sentinels of gods who wander round us.

"Not me,—go quickly, wanton, with another, and hasten like a chariot-wheel to meet him." (Rig. X. 10, 8; A. V. XVIII. I, 9).

The epithets (1) wise, (2) holy, (3) skilled in sacrifices, (4) and furtherers of praise songs are evidently applicable only to the priests. The reason why spies were recruited from among the Brahmans is not also far to seek. The epithet, holy, sacred in person so as not to be hurt either by friend or foe, supplies the reason. If spies had not been recruited in the first instance from a class of persons who, in virtue of their learning and capacity to perform sacrifices correctly so as to secure good and avert evil, were sincerely regarded as sacred in person and granted the six immunities referred to in Lecture IV above, it is probable that the system of espionage itself would have hardly lasted long and served its purpose. It cannot be denied that human society is highly indebted to the priestly class of its own make for its existence and its progress. Though spies were recruited from all classes of people and messengers and envoys only from among the priestly class during the times of Kautilya[177] (Buddhist Jatakas, VI. 528), the above Vedic passage goes to show that during the Vedic period Brahmans alone served as spies, and that their person was regarded as inviolate. The duty of these sacred spies was not merely to visit every spot, and find out him who was bent on evil and keep guard over fields and plants (Rig. VII. 61, 3), but also to catch hold of criminals who might commit social or religious wrongs. Hence under the apprehension of these spies Yama rejects the love of his sister Yami and asks her to find out another husband for herself. (Rig. X. 10, 1-16.)

While in virtue of their personal inviolability, the Brahmans in their capacity as spies served not merely to police the Aryan settlements but also to act as envoys and messengers in the settlement of international or intertribal affairs, during the Vedic period, recruitment of spies at later times seems to have been made from other classes also and especially from those who were poor and destitute and thus, depended on the government for their subsistence[178] when the expansion of states from petty settlements into large kingdoms required an organised system of espionage, on a large scale. No political department seems to have given so much trouble to ancient statesmen as the organisation of the institution of spies so as to be serviceable to the state. It was a department that was expected to serve the state in various capacities. While its primary or principal duty was evidently to supply the king and his minister or ministers with reliable information touching the conduct of public servants in carrying out the work entrusted to them and of the people at large in their dealings with the government or with each other

---

[177] Artha, I. 16.

[178] Artha., I. 12.

among themselves, it was also required to train its spies in various capacities; spies to act as cultivators, traders, ascetics, astrologers, wizards, foretellers, dancers, players actors, cooks, sweetmeat-makers, poisoners, medical men, cowherds, milkmen, milkmaids, pedlars, shop-keepers, ventners, sellers of cooked flesh and cooked rice, artisans, handicraftsmen, goldsmiths, silversmiths, mendicant men or women, sorcerers, prostitutes, washermen, weavers and men of as many profession as were found in any civilized society of those times.

Spies were classed into five groups.

(1) Idlers or spies with no definite occupation or profession except that of closely and pryingly watching the movements of men and women and of ascertaining the motive of their actions.

(2) Foretellers acquainted with palmistry, astrology and other sorts of learning of the same kind and engaged in detecting crimes.

(3) Spies with the profession of agriculture.

(4) Spies with trade as their profession.

(5) Ascetics with shaved head and braided hair, pretending to be engaged in practising austerities.

In addition to these five classes or Samsthas as they were called by Kautilya there were also three more groups, such as, (1) Satrins or apprentices, (2) Tikshnas or firebrands, murderers with deadly weapons in their hands and (3) Rasadas, poisoners. These three groups were called wandering spies in virtue of their constant touring through different countries. To assist spies of all these seven groups and also to carry out the work of espionage independently by themselves there were also women spies, such as mendicant women, cooks, nurses and prostitutes.[179]

---

[179] Arthasastra I. 11; 1

Of these eight classes, the first five were under the management of five offices or institutions independent of each other and with large landed estates or manufactories worked by themselves for their maintenance without entailing no revenue-expenditure on the state. In other words, they seem to have been self-supporting institutions combining in one the duties of four of our modern departments, the Police, the Intelligence, the Educational, and the Poorhouse.

The other three classes called wandering spies seem to have been under the supervision of the government itself, *i.e.*, the king and his ministers, and having no communication with or knowledge of, the work carried on by the five institutes. When the information gathered from these three different sources, *i.e.*, the five institutes, the wandering spies, and women spies was of the same kind, it was considered reliable and steps were taken to act up accordingly. If the information supplied by one or two sources did not tally with that gathered from the other two or more sources, the spies concerned were doomed and severely punished, dismissed or hanged, so as to secure the safety of the king and his kingdom. So delicate and dangerous was the work of the system of espionage that under its poisonous breath and sting neither private citizens nor public servants could be sure of the safety of their person and property. Hence in order to avoid this risk to life and property, great caution seems to have been taken in giving credence to these tales and no credence seems to have been given to them unless those tales issuing from three different sources not in touch with each other were exactly of the same type.

In addition to these spies and superior to them in rank and duty, there were also envoys, messengers and Ubhaya Vetanas or Recipients of salaries from two states, who acted partly as spies and partly as ambassadors doing the duty of extradition of criminals and traitors and of observing the treaties of peace and war in the courts of foreign kings. Recipients of salaries from two states were however required to leave their wives and children as hostages in pledge of their trustworthy character under the custody of kings by whom they were missioned to reside in the court of their allies. Accustomed as we are with the press, post, telegraph, telephone and other organs supplying both the government and the public with reliable information to act upon, with no risk worth mentioning, it may seem strange that ancient states had succeeded in accomplishing their works with tolerable safety on the strength of the information of untrustworthy spies or news writers, as they were called by Megasthenes and Greek writers. The times needed such an institution and there was no other means to get at the truth. Indispensable as was this kind of intelligence department to the state for all its information, there is evidence to believe that kings had no reason to regret for the trust they placed in their informants. It is stated that Arrion[180] was assured that the reports sent in were always true, and that no Indian could be accused of lying. Though historians of India are inclined to doubt the strict accuracy of the statements of Greek writers in this connection[181] the importance attached to the institute of espionage in the Arthasastra and the daily audience given by the king to the spies as one of his daily duties goes to show that it was a trustworthy department and was probably more reliable than some of our newspapers with their party and racial prejudice. Thus though its trustworthiness

---

[180] Vincent Smith's History of India, 2nd Edition, pp. 127 & 135.

[181] Vincent Smith's History of India, 2nd Edition, p. 128.

as a news agency cannot be doubted, the moral aspect of its work done in friendly or inimical states, as specified in Books XI, XII, XIII, XIV, of the Arthasastra, may however be questioned and condemned as open to the objection of moralists. The employment of fiery spies to murder in cold blood a seditious minister or his relation and to arrest the survivors on the charge of murder imputed to them,[182] or to exact money from the people under the pretext of undertaking remedial measures against ominous occurrences, or to concoct false charges against disloyal persons so as to expose them to capital punishments,[183] or to administer poison in foodstuffs, water, milk, wine and other articles of diet and beverage so as to bring about death of an enemy's subjects by hundreds and thousands[184] or to set fire to an enemy's palace or capital town so as to bring about his death, or to slaughter an enemy's army by using explosives and poisonous smokes, as stated in Book XIV of the Arthasastra, are undoubtedly unrighteous acts that are severely condemned by Bana, the author of Kadambari, in the following words :—

"Is there anything that is righteous for those for whom the science of Kautilya, merciless in its attempts, and precepts, rich in cruelty, is an authority; whose teacher are priests habitually hard-hearted with the practice of witchcraft; to whom ministers, always inclined to deceive others, are councillors; whose desire is always inclined for the goddess of wealth that has been cast away by thousands of kings; who are devoted to the application of destructive sciences; and to whom brothers, affectionate with natural cordial love, are fit victims to be murdered?"

(Kadambari, p. 109, Bombay Education Society Press.)

---

182 Artha., V. 1.

183 *Ibid*, V. 2.

184 *Ibid*, VII. 17.

Though intrigue, espionage, poison, fire, cold-blooded murder and other measures of the same kind proposed and employed by Kautilya with the set purpose of building an empire, *i.e.*, the empire of the Mauryas beginning with Chandragupta on the ruins of the ancient Nāndas tend to make him a cruel tyrant or tyrannical minister bereft of moral principles, of right and wrong and of justice and injustice, still there is reason to believe that concerning the administration of a territory, inherited, recovered, or conquered, he was a benevolent despot always devoted to the cause of righteousness and justice. This is what he himself has stated regarding the administration of kingdoms in general. (Artha., XIII. 5) :—

" He should initiate the observance of all those customs, which though righteous and practised by others, are not observed in his own country, and give no room for the practice of whatever is unrighteous, though observed by others."

Evidently Kautilya belongs to that school of politicians whose policy is to justify the means by the noble end sought to be achieved. Even now there are a number of persons who consider it within the province of justice to rob Peter and pay Paul, provided Paul is admitted a god or an angel, and who, with the object of making a religious or charitable endowment, do not hesitate to confiscate justly or unjustly the property of a person of infamous or unrighteous character or to levy blackmail from lowcaste wealthy persons for some religious cause.

Evidently Kautilya seems to have belonged to this school of thinkers who, though few in numbers now, appear to have formed a majority in those far-off days inspite of the prevalence of puritanic forms of moral thoughts based upon the humanitarian principles of Jainism and Buddhism. Strengthened with this thought Kautilya seems to have considered himself justified in planning, developing and successfully employing the five means to carry out his policy of building an empire with Vedic religion and Vedic sacrifices restored to their former glory.

Slender as might seem the means relied upon by Kautilya to carry out his ambitious project of building an empire on religious basis, there were also other means which, besides giving considerable strength to his huge army of spies, rendered the country quite ripe for his political experiment. Though morally strong under the influence of the humanitarian religion of the Jainas and the Buddhists, the Military organisation of the kingdoms seems to have been too weak to withstand an organised attack by enemies. As admitted[185] by Aśoka, the non-Aryan states were naturally addicted to evil-doing and were waiting for an opportunity to pounce upon the helpless Buddhist kingdom either for plunder or revenge. There is reason to believe that like Asoka who is stated[186] to have deprived sixty thousand Brahmans of their daily royal bounty and entertained in their place an equal number of Buddhist monks, there were Jaina and Buddhist kings before him, who had treated the Brahmans with no less disrespect than Asoka himself. It can be more easily imagined than described how the despised and neglected Brahmans were more eagerly waiting for an opportunity to avenge themselves upon the Buddhists than the wild tribes and non-Aryan states in their habitual thirst for plunder and territory. The Brahman politicians of the Buddhist period seem to have drawn upon these enemies of Buddhism for their huge army of spies and soldiers to constitute the five means to build an empire. Absorbed in their

---

185 Edict XIII.

186 Vincent Smith's Asoka, p. 162.

constant meditation to conquer the inimical passions, the Buddhist kings seem to have lost sight of these external enemies that were planning for their downfall.

The other two means which formed part of Kautilya's empire-building policy are the reinstatement of conquered kings in the whole or part of their own territory on feudal tenure and the sale of waste lands for colonization to such rich persons as were found unfitted by their character and temper to establish themselves as rulers over their settlements. In the view of Kautilya these were only makeshifts, made use of in the interest of an imperial sovereign state rather than the interest of the feudatory chief or the colonizer, both of whom were expected to come to grief in their attempts to fulfil the terms of the agreement entered upon by them with the suzerain power. This is what Kautilya says regarding a feudatory Chief (XIII. 5) :—

"Whoever of the enemy's family is capable to wrest the conquered territory and is taking shelter in a wild tract on the border, often harassing the conqueror, should be provided with a sterile portion of territory with a fourth part of a fertile tract on the condition of supplying to the conqueror a fixed amount of money and fixed number of troops, in raising which he may incur the displeasure of the people and may be destroyed by them."

Similarly the colonizer was also expected to perish in his attempts, contributing to the prosperity of his suzerain lord. In reply to his teacher's objection that an indiscreet colonizer may sometimes betray the weak points of the suzerain lord himself, Kautilya says that "just as he betrays the weak points, so also does he facilitate his own destruction by the suzerain lord.[1]

---

[187] Artha., VII. 11.

The peculiar feature of Kautilya's empire-building policy is evidently the utilization of all possible resources to expand and aggrandise the imperial power and the employment of correct means to get rid of all possible enemies, either internal or external without exposing the emperor and his ministers to any form of public calumny.

LECTURE IX

THEOCRATIC DESPOTISM

It had been made clear from the foregoing lectures how India had passed from tribal democracy to elective monarchy with priestly domination in some cases and to government by clans or to oligarchy in others; and how elective monarchy gave place to hereditary monarchy with or without priestly supremacy; and how under the influence of the humanitarian doctrines of Jainism and Buddhism, hereditary monarchy freed itself from its thraldom to Brahman hieracracy and took rest for some time or for some centuries in the paradise of the Ganas or Gentes of the Jainas or of the Sanghas or brotherhood of the Buddhist Dhammachakka or Empire of righteousness with their numberless Vasatis or Bastis and Viharas or Monasteries.

Now under the peaceful revolution brought about by Kautilya and other politicians of his times, it does not appear that the question of a form of government suitable to India and her people, especially her Vedic priests or Brahmans was left to its own evolutionary solution without interference or meddling under religious bias. It is probable that if she had been left to herself or if the turn which she had taken in her political movement under the influence of Buddhism had been preserved undisturbed, she would have certainly arrived under a limited monarchy subject to popular will or under an oligarchy or government by Kulas or clans like that of the Sakyas, Vrijikas, Mallakas, Mudrakas, Kukuras, Kurus, Panchalas and others.[188] But her politicians

[188] Artha., I. 17; XI. 1; Rhys David's Buddhist India, pp. 2, 19; Jatakas, I. 504, IV. 145; V. 413; VI. 238, 575-7.

did meddle with it, as their predecessors did on a number of occasions before with a set purpose or motive. Now the motive was to put down Jainism and Buddhism and to restore Brahmanism to its former glory, though somewhat dwindled.

While the Buddhists were quite earnest in their desire to perpetuate the principles of justice, charity, and brotherhood and were inclined to prefer the old republican or rather oligarchical form of government after their ideal Dhammachakka, Empire of Righteousness in which all had equal treatment, rights and privileges, the politicians of the Kautilya period were for a government in which the Vedic priestly oligarchy had special privileges granted to it so as to excite no clannish prejudice or hatred as before. They knew very well that in the face of Buddhist opposition, the Brahmans could not revive their claim to the old [illegible] immunities now lost to them. If they had to be given at all any preponderancy in the body politic, it should then evidently be in some modified form. They could not be entirely exempted from punishment for offences as before.

As a mark of respect to their learning, piety and penance, a scale of punishments based upon class or caste distinctions seems to have been devised making the punishment inflicted on the Brahman class decidedly less than that meted out to others.[189] Instead of exempting the Brahman class as a whole from taxes and tolls on the lands and merchandise possessed by them, a new custom of granting to particular individuals Brahmadeyika lands free from tax and with restrictions to the right of sale and mortgage seems to have been invented during the same period.[190] In some cases Brahmans seem to have been

---

[189] Artha., III. 18, 19.

[190] Artha., II. 1.

allowed to enjoy free grants of lands made to temples and Mutts,[191] after the manner of Jaina and Buddhist kings who seem to have given rich endowments to their Bustis and Viharas or Buddhist monasteries Instead of clothing and feeding the Brahmans as a whole in all places at the expense of public revenue in satisfaction of their old claim to exemption from cold, heat, thirst, and hunger, special feeding houses after the Buddhist alms-houses seem to have been established in a number of sacred places by way of manifesting devotion to gods and faith in religion and charity. Thus though even hermits too, had been compelled to pay taxes and suffer punishment for offences like others[192] the indirect way of helping Brahmans as a whole by richly endowing their temples, Mutts, and other religious institutions in the name of religion appears to be the invention of the politicians of the Kautilya period. Following the Jaina and the Buddhist monks who superintended the feeding of the poor in their richly endowed alms-houses and monasteries, the Brahman hermits and ascetics began to possess rich landed estates attached to their temples and Mutts and to feed Brahmans on all days,—a custon quite opposed to the express text of the Upanishads.[193] Though they are forbidden to receive presents and own lands, they seem to have begun to argue following the precedent of the Jainas and the Buddhists that it was no sin to superintend the land of gods and to feed the poor with the sole aim of pleasing the gods worshipped by them in the interests of the king and his kingdom.

Thus having found out an easy way of helping the Brahmans and of reviving their Vedic religion, the

[191] Artha., II. 1.

[192] Artha., I. 13.

[193] Sannyasopanishad, Chap. 1.

politicians of the Kautilya period seem to have entertained no doubts as to the particular form of government that would answer their purpose of helping the cause of the Brahmans. Neither democracy with power vested in the hands of even the low-caste persons, nor oligarchy under the sway of apostates and atheists would be of any help to Brahmanism. The wayward hereditary monarchies of the Kshatriyas hated the Brahmans, renounced the Vedas and embraced Jainism or Buddhism at their pleasure. Hence the Kshatriyas who were found wanting in their attachment to Brahmanism had to be replaced by others in the monarchical system of government. Though Kautilya had opposed the opinion of Bharadvaja[104] that given an opportunity, Brahman ministers might do well to replace the Kshatriya rule by Brahman rule, and preferred to preserve the old order founded on popular will, he seems to have given it up and preferred wild chiefs of Sudra origin like Chandragupta. Different as are the accounts given in the Puranas and other literary works regarding the descent of Chandragupta, they all agree in making him a Sudra Kautilya is made to call him a Vrishala in the Mudrarakshasa. According to the Vishnu and other Purans the Kshatriya race came to an end with Mahapadma, the last Kshatriya king and after him the 'kings of the earth' were of Sudra origin.[105] But there is evidence to prove that though in the terrible conflict that ensued between the Brahmans and the Kshatriyas, the ruling race had dwindled to a great extent, there still existed a few Kshatriya kings such as Pushyamitra Samudragupta, Kumaragupta and others who were al regarded to be of the Kshatriya descent, entitled to

---

[104] Artha., V. 6.

[105] Vishnu, IV. 24.

perform the horse sacrifice.[196] Still it cannot however be denied that smarting with the pain of ill-treatment by the hostile kings of the Kshatriya race, the Brahmans sought the help of the wild chiefs of Sudra descent against the effeminate Buddhist kings and that the chiefs of forest tribes availed themselves of the good opportunity to establish themselves as kings in many of the Aryan kingdoms. This is confirmed by the following passages of the Vishnupurana (LV. 24) :—

"In Magadha, a sovereign named Visvasphatika, will establish other tribes ; he will extirpate the Kshatriya race and elevate fishermen, barbarians, Yadus, Pulindas, and Brahmans to power. The nine Nagas will reign in Padmavati, Kantipuri and Madhura. A prince named Devarakshita will reign in a city on the seashore over the Kosals, Odras, Pundrakas and Tamraliptas.—Men of the three tribes, but degraded, and Abhiras, and Sudras will occupy Saurashtra, Avanti, Sura, Arbuda, and Marubhumi ; and Sudras, and outcastes, and barbarians will be masters of the banks of the Indus, Darvika, the Chandrabhaga and Kashmira."

Thus almost all Aryan kingdoms from the Himalayas in the North to the Vindhya range in the South and from the Indus in the West to the mouth of the Ganges in the East seem to have fallen again one after another into the hands of Dravidian races in the conflict between the Brahmans and the Buddhist Kshatriyas during the post-Buddhistic period, while to the south of the Vindhya mountains the old Dravidians, the Cholas, Pandyas, and the Keralaputras had all along continued to rule over their respective kingdoms unmolested and undisturbed by the Aryans. Historians of India seem to have scarcely

---

196 Vincent Smith's History of India, pp. 273, 284, 287.

noticed how as a substratum of the revival of Brahmanism there appeared at the same time a real revival of Dravidian rule in the whole of India. How far in this reassertion of Dravidian rule mutual compromise between the two civilizations, Dravidian and Aryan, was effected so far as their respective social, religious, and political customs are concerned, is a question that deserves careful study and investigation. It is probable that temple worship and car-processions in which Dravidian kings acted as the servants of gods worshipped in the temples were largely substituted for the Vedic animal sacrifices and that all religious establishments were now placed under the supervision of the Brahmans.

The Brahmans seem to have considered themselves quite justified in the revolutionary step they had taken to replace the hostile Kshatriya rule by Dravidian rule. Accordingly in reply to the question of Yudhisthira as to "who would protect the Brahmans and their Vedas, if all the Kshatriyas proved hostile to the Brahmans; and what then should be the duty of the Brahmans and who would be their refuge," Bhisma is made to say in the Mahabharata as follows[197] :—

" By penances, by Brahmacharya, by weapons, and by might, applied with or without the aid of deceit, the Kshatriyas should be subjugated. If the Kshatriya misconducts himself, especially towards the Brahmans, the Vedas will subjugate them. The *Kshatriyas have sprung from the Brahmans*..............All persons should take up arms for the sake of the Brahmans. Those brave persons that fight for the Brahmans attain to these felicitous regions in heaven that are reserved for persons that have always studied the Vedas with attention..................I bow to

---

[197] Santi Rajadharmaparva, Chap. 78.

them and blessed be they that thus lay down their lives in seeking to chastise the enemies of the Brahmans............. Be he a *Sudra* or *be he a member of any other order*, he that becomes a raft on a raftless current or a means of crossing where means there are none, certainly deserves respect in every way. That person that dispels the fears of others always deserves respect. What use is there of bulls that would not bear burdens or of kine that would not yield milk or of a wife that is barren? Similarly, what need is there for a king that is not competent to grant protection?"

Again in Chapter 123 of the Rajadharmaparva Bhisma is made to say quoting the words of one called Kamanda in the same tune as follows :—

"If the king does not restrain those wicked men of sinful conduct, all good subjects then live in fear of him like the inmates of a room in which a snake has concealed itself. The subjects do not follow such a king. Brahmans and all pious persons also act in the same way. As a consequence the king falls into great danger and ultimately deserves destruction itself. Men learned in the scriptures have indicated the following means for checking sin. The king should always devote himself to the study of the three Vedas; he should respect the Brahmans and do good offices unto them. He should be devoted to righteousness. He should wait upon high-minded Brahmans adorned with the virtue of forgiveness."

Having thus clearly defined the position and the privileges of the Brahmans under the revived Dravidian rule, the politicians of the post-Kautilya period seem to have been equally careful in defining the rights and prerogatives of the monarchs also in the reformed polity. From the dawn of the Vedic period down to the commencement of the Kautilya period, no attempt seems to have been made to divinize a ruler's person or his rights. Such Vedic records as refer to his expulsion and restoration, on the contrary, go to show that he was regarded merely as a man under the power of the priestly oligarchy on the one hand and of the people's assembly on the other. The custom of Niyoga or deputing a neighbouring king to beget a prince on a sonless widowed queen[198] seems to have rendered such a claim inconsistent with his birth. In the theory of Kautilya, the king is merely an accident : he may be high-born or base-born,[199] a feudatory chief[200] or a colonizer,[201] destined to be either a prince or a pauper. So long as he is a king, he is a rewarder like Indra and punisher like Yama in virtue of his possession of Indra-Yamasthana[202] ; so he deserves respect. Whatever might be his birth, he should adhere to the customs of the Aryas and the rules of classes and religious divisions.[203] He must be guided by his Brahman ministers and must follow the precepts of the Sastras.[204] Kautilya seems to have regarded the Sudras among the Aryas and contrasted them with the Mlechchas, or non-Aryan people.[205] It follows therefore that he considered even Sudra kings as Aryan kings practising Aryan customs. As caste-system with its exclusive rights of connubium and commensality has not as yet made its appearance during the Kautilya period, it follows that any one could then become a Brahman or a Kshatriya or a Vaisya in virtue of exercising the duties assigned to those respective classes. Whatever might be

[198] Artha., V. 6.

[199] Artha., XIII.

[200] Artha., VIII. 11.

[201] Artha., I. 13.

[202] *Ibid*, I. 1. 3. 6.

[203] *Ibid*, I. 9.

[204] *Ibid*, III. 13.

[205] Artha., I. 9; VI. 1.

the opinion of scholars on this particular question regarding the existence or absence of rigid caste system in the fourth century B.C., this much is certain that neither during the Vedic period nor in the times of Kautilya, divine birth or right of kings seems to have been thought of. Then it was either elective or hereditary monarchy entirely under the power of the priestly oligarchy and the peoples' assembly; or it was a republic of clans or the Dhamma-chakka or the kingdom of righteousness of the Buddhists. During the times of the empire-building politicians when the old Dravidians were given facilities to regain their royal power, it was again the Brahman priest[206] and the assembly of ministers[207] (Mantriparishad) that were expected to exercise some check over the revived Dravidian rule.

This unfirm yet brave upstart, a mere flag in the hands of his ministers, as termed by Kautilya,[207] seems to have been looked upon as being too low-born to fill up the high place he was called to occupy. To make up for this want the later politicians of India seem to have invented and developed the idea of divine birth and right of kings as *sine qua non* to royal power. Accordingly the king is declared as an incarnation of deities by Manu and other later Smriti writers. This is what Manu says in V. 96-7 :

"A king is an incarnation of the eight guardian deities of the world, the Moon, the Fire, the Sun, the Wind, Indra, the Lords of Wealth and Water (Kubera and Varuna), and Yama. Because the king is pervaded by those lords of the world, no impurity is ordained for him; for purity and impurity of mortals is caused and removed by those lords of the world."

---

[206] Artha., I. 9; VI. 1.

[207] *Ibid*, V. 6.

Again in VII. 4-8 Manu says in support of the divine birth and right of kings more explicitly in the following words :—

"Taking (for the purpose of creating a king) eternal particles of Indra, of the Wind, of Yama, of the Sun, of Fire, of Varuna, of the Moon, and of the Lord of Wealth (Kubera), the Lord created a king. Because a king has been formed of particles of those lords of the gods, he therefore surpasses all created beings in lustre. Like the Sun he burns eyes and hearts, nor can any body on earth even gaze on him......Even an infant king must not be despised (from the idea) that he is a mere mortal, for he is a great deity in human form."

This picture of a king being a deity in human form, as drawn by Manu in the above verses, should be contrasted with the picture of a king, portrayed as a mere mortal in the Vedas and the Arthasastra. I can conceive no other reason for this sudden change of ideas about the right of kings than the necessity of hiding the low birth of restored Dravidian kings of the Buddhistic period and of strengthening their royal power so as to be able to guard the interest of the Brahmans. This is purely a Brahmanic conception consistent with their theistic religion. Neither Jainism nor Buddhism could possibly entertain such theistic notions consistent with their agnostic faith, or the kingdom of righteousness based upon the equality of individual rights, be he a prince or pauper. While in the Brahmanic conception of political justice or injustice, the king was held answerable to god Varuna for all his unjust acts and was accordingly compelled to pay a fine to Varuna and distribute it among Brahmans in expiation of his wrong deeds[208] the Buddhists seem to have held the king

---

[208] Artha., IV. 13.

directly responsible to the people for all his acts and taken the law in their own hands in dealing with an erring king. Accordingly we are told in the Jatakas [209] of kings put to death for outraging a woman (II. 1222-3), for ingratitude (I. 326), for endangering life (III. 574), for attempting to make a sacrifice of a prince, or reprimanded and corrected (VI. 155) for developing cannibalistic tastes (V. 470), or for not taking steps to avert a drought, as narrated in the Vessantara Jataka (487-8) or for causing famines by his unrighteous acts (II. 124; 368). This kind of treatment of kings on naturalistic basis or on a footing of equality with ordinary people would by no means be in harmony with class or individual superiority and special births and prerogatives. Hence in the interests of their own privileges and consistently with their theistic conception, the Brahmans seem to have divinized royalty irrespective of its birth and race.

There is no doubt this innovation rendered monarchy still more despotic and freed it from all popular check it had till then. Still the same religion which elevated the monarch and enabled him to enjoy his privileges, besides conferring them on castes and creeds in his own interests seems to have been used also to prevent him from all acts unrighteous in the view of the Brahmans. In addition to the theistic threats and dangers which were used to keep him at bay, there were also political threats and dangers due to court intrigue which kept him in constant apprehension of danger to his position and life. Thus though the credit of having established a theocratic despotism with these safe checks is clearly due to the politicians of the post-Buddhistic period, still, if deeply considered, the credit or blame for this

[209] See Principal Subba Rao's the Jatakas and Indian Polity.

change seems to have rested with people themselves. It may be taken for granted that no statesman or politician can rise far above the circumstances of his time and succeed in instituting a good or bad measure against the will of the people at large. He must take into his consideration the prevailing sentiments and views of the people before taking steps to introduce any change in the social, religious, or political conditions of the people. If the time is ripe for his experiment, he will succeed in it, but if unripe, he will certainly be thwarted in his attempts and will utterly fail. Hence it is the intellectual and spiritual advancement of the people themselves that is responsible for the success or failure of any social or political change introduced among them.

The early Dravidian settlers of India who, consistent with their totemistic religious views, worshipped stones, trees, rivers, serpents and wild beasts seem to have been utterly dissatisfied with the high morality of the agnostic humanitarian religion of the Jainas and the Buddhists and gladly welcomed the theistic religion of the Brahmans who in their turn took the opportunity to enlarge and bring to the forefront their Tantric and Agamic cult of Atharvanic origin. At the same time the Brahmans seem to have given up the old customs of intermarriage and interdining with other classes and reformed and recast their religion on philosophic basis, as taught in the Upanishads. While the Tantric cult with its animal offerings is termed Vamachara, left-hand practice, the philosophic religion of the Upanishads was called the Dakshinachara or right-hand practice.

Thus the chief features of the Brahmanic revival are: (1) the revival of the Dravidians, and (2) their Tantric religion in Brahmanic garb, (3) the revival of Sanskrit literature and language, (4) establishment of theocratic despotism with theistic checks and Brahmanic power at the background, (5) decline and fall of Jainism and Buddhism, and (6) the formation of castes. It should be noted that attended though they might appear with sanguinary deeds, all these changes deserve to be termed evolutionary, having for their basis a general permanent mental change among the people at large, as contrasted with revolutionary reforms based upon a temporary whimsical change in the mental look-out of a few individuals. While a revolutionary change disappears with its violent authors, evolutionary changes persist till a general change occurs in the sentiments and views of the people at large due to education or to the preaching of reformers.

LECTURE X

THE CONDITION OF THE PEOPLE, INTELLECTUAL, SPIRITUAL AND ECONOMICAL

In the rapid bird's-eye view we have taken of the most important changes that had taken place in the social, religious, and political condition of the Aryan settlers in India during the long stretches of time commencing from the Vedic period down to the fall of Buddhism, I have dwelt at length only on the political changes, reserving the intellectual and economical vicissitudes in the condition of the people for consideration in a separate paper. Properly speaking, there can be no political change unless it is preceded by vast intellectual, spiritual and economical changes in the condition of the people. Attention has already been drawn to the radical changes which Jainism and Buddhism had wrought out on the social, moral and religious views of the people, engendering equally important political changes in consequence. The intellectual and economical changes that were interwoven with the above changes were no less in magnitude. The marvellous progress which Vedic and Buddhist India has made in education is so well known and treated of in detail by so many learned scholars that any attempt on my part to talk of the Vedic poets, the authors of the Brahmans and the Kalpasutras, the grammarians, the logicians, the philosophers, the epic writers, the poets and others is merely a sheer waste of time. Instead of wasting my time in boasting of India's educational monuments and pyramids, I think I may do better in drawing your attention to some of the broad principles which characterised the educational policy of the Brahmanic Jaina and the Buddhist hierarchy or clergy. It is to be noted that ancient India knew neither government schools and colleges nor aided institutions with professors paid for their teaching and students paying for their learning. Education was free and for all. It was a sin to sell or purchase education. It was as a sacred duty of the student to go to his family-priest or any other teacher in quest of learning as it was of the teacher to impart education on the subject sought for. There were no boarding houses. The student had to beg his food and remain a bachelor as long as he studied. It was the duty of the householders also to give a handful of cooked rice to each of the begging students, however large the number might be. Completion of education marked the period of marriage.

Sacred as was the duty of teaching and learning, no subject, whether Vedic or Puranic, seems to have been considered so sacred as to preclude it on caste considerations; for there were no castes in Vedic and Buddhistic India. Women and Sudras who had been precluded later from Vedic studies had during the Vedic period to learn at least such Vedic hymns as they had to recite on occasions of sacrifices.[210] Nishadas and Vratyas had the right to perform sacrifices and learn the necessary sacrificial hymns and formulas. In spite of Badarayana's ingenious explanation of the word Sudra[211] as an epithet indicating grief in Janasruti in IV. 2, 3 of the Chhandogyo-panishad, I am inclined to believe that Janasruti was a king of the Sudra class and that Raikva, a Brahman philosopher of the time, had no hesitation or scruples in teaching him the Vedantic philosophy, as required. When at a later period

---

[210] Asval. Grihya, III. 4, 4.

[211] Vedanta Sutras, I. 3, 34.

women and Sudras were precluded under the baneful influence of castes from the study of the Vedas and Upanishads in the original, Puranic and other literary works embodying the sacred ideas of the Vedas and the Upanishads were written specially in their interests. Likewise the Jainas and the Buddhists taught and wrote their religion and morality in the Prakritic or Dravidian languages solely for the benefit of the people at large. While higher education was imparted through the medium of either Sanskrit or Prakrit, primary and secondary education seem to have been carried on in the vernacular languages of the learners themselves. Sanskrit was, as it still now is, the literary language of the Brahmans and Prakrit of the Magadhi type the spoken and literary language of the Jainas and the Buddhists. Neither the Brahmans nor the Jainas and the Buddhists seem to have been sparing in their efforts to improve the vocabulary of the innumerable languages of the continent of India so as to render each of them a fit vehicle to convey higher scientific ideas. The magnitude of the trouble which the Brahmans, the Jainas and the Buddhists had taken to improve the various Dravidian languages can be easily perceived if an attempt is made to reduce the list of the words proper to each of the vernacular by removing the huge number of Sanskrit and Prakrit words imported into each. This task, gigantic though it may be, will be of immense help in preparing an estimate of the comparative indebtedness of the civilizations, the Dravidian and Aryan, to each other. It is likely that without caring for such troublesome questions as Eastern Education, Western Education, National Education and the like which are more likely easily asked than answered, the Dravidians earnestly took themselves to study and assimilate the new scientific ideas of the Aryan invaders. Thus in employing two languages as the medium of instruction, one for higher and another for primary education, modern India has evidently adopted the same procedure that ancient India had of old followed.

But so far as the curriculum of studies and the method of improving education are concerned, ancient India seems to have excelled modern India. Her curriculum was simpler and more adapted to the needs of the student, while her method of imparting education was catechistical and quite suited to the varying intellectual calibre, æsthetic tendency or aptitude of the learners. The primary course expected to be completed before the student was invested with the sacred thread consisted of reading, writing (*lipi*) and arithmetic (*samkhyana*); while the secondary and higher course comprised: (1) the Vedas, together with *angas*, such as phonetics, ceremonial injunctions, grammar, glossary of words, prosody, and astronomy, (2) Sankhya Yoga, and Lokayata, (3) Agriculture, cattle-breeding, and trade, (4) and the science of polity,[212] (5) Military arts and history, specially for the Kshatriyas.

While the subjects of the primary course seem to have been compulsory, it appears that students were allowed the option of selecting one, many or all of the subjects in the secondary and higher courses according to their individual capacity and taste. Though the art of writing, which, as I have endeavoured to show elsewhere, was an indigenous invention, was known in India so far back as the 17th century before Christ, manuscripts available for study seem to have been very few. Hence students seem to have been obliged to depend on the retentive capacity of their memory for their success in learning. It appears that the student was taught a verse, half of a verse or quarter of a verse or an aphorism or two to

[212] Artha., I. 5.

begin with and that when he was found to have digested its meaning and the reasoning by "hearing over and over again what he could not clearly understand,[213] he was allowed to continue his studies in the same way till the subject was completed. The one excellent feature of the curriculum, worth of being noticed, is the inclusion in it of such most useful subjects as agriculture, cattle-breeding, and trade. Whether our modern curriculum may or may not be so recast as to contain more of agricultural or industrial arts and less of geography and history both in the primary and secondary courses, is a question that seems to be deserving of consideration by educationists.

It appears strange that, in spite of her despotic rule, lack of easy communication, and anarchical tendency of the people addicted to constant plotting against well-established governments, which rendered it more necessary to prohibit the study of political and military sciences in those times than in modern India with her standing army, well-organised police and other powerful protective means, ancient India included in her curriculum of studies such dangerous subjects as political and military sciences to be studied by all at their option.

Another excellent characteristic feature of her educational policy was her catechistical method of teaching as efficiently as possible a fixed number of students one after another by a single teacher. There can be no difference of opinion on the defect of the modern method of entrusting to a single lecturer or professor the work of teaching to classes consisting of more than 50 to 100 students of varying mental calibre. The evils of imparting education on class-system seem to have been felt even so far back as the 7th or 8th century A.D. and the utter failure of instructing

[213] Artha., I. 5.

a class of even three students is thus depicted by Bhavabhuti in the second Act of his Uttararama Charita (Act II. 4):—

"A teacher imparts knowledge equally to the intelligent and dull: neither does he sharpen the grasping power of one, nor blunt that of another. Yet as regards the result there is vast difference. It is this: a clear gem has the power of receiving light and reflecting it, but a clod of earth has not."

It is matter for delight that unlike our modern orthodox community, ancient Aryans held in high esteem all kinds of education, no matter from what source and through what medium it had to be acquired. While they were ready to impart to Sudras and women whatever they knew,[214] they were not at all loth to supplement their study by learning whatever the latter in their turn could impart to them. This is confirmed by the following statement made by Apastamba in his Dharma Sutra (II. 11, 29, 11-12):—

"The knowledge which Sudras and women possess is the completion of all study. They declare that this knowledge is a supplement of the Atharvaveda.[215] According to Haradatta, and the commentators on Apastamba, the knowledge which women and Sudras possess is dancing, music, and other branches of the Arthasastra. Since medicine and witch-craft form the subject matter of the Atharvaveda to a large extent, it is probable that women and Sudras had as much knowledge of these subjects as they have even now.

Another excellent feature of the education system of ancient India is the rigorous discipline to which students

---

[214] Asval. Grih., III. 4, 4.

[215] Manu, II. 238-242.

were subjected in all their movements, social, religious, and educational. No period in the history of India seems to have been more uncongenial for the formation of individual character than Vedic and post-Vedic age with its promiscuity among women, laxity of marriage tie, religious free thinking, espionage, and anarchical tendency among the people at large ; and yet no system of education was more adapted for the exercise of rigorous discipline over the conduct of students and for the formation of character than the system of Gurukulavasam, according to which the student was required to live with the teacher and observe the rules of the education code to the very letter.[216] Character seems to have been considered as a moral trait of personal bearing partly inherited and partly acquired.[217] In spite of their attachment to the theory of political expediency or the employment of means, fair or foul, to achieve an end with no attention to its moral aspect, Kautilya and other politicians seem to have considered character as *sine-qua-non* of the well-being of mankind, not merely social and religious, but also political well-being. In the view of Kautilya lack of character in a man, be he a king or prince, priest or prime minister, servant or spy, spelled ruin to the whole state. Hence not content with the usual four texts of character, bearing on the four human pursuits, virtue, wealth, love, and spirituality, as narrated in the Arthasastra (I. 10), Kautilya advises the king to let loose a swarm of spies to watch and report on the evil deeds of men and women, irrespective of their class, creed and occupation.

There is no doubt that there were special treatises on agriculture, industry and trade, which formed part of the curriculum of studies. They are termed Krishitantra,

---

[216] Apa., I. 1, 2 and I. 2, 3.

[217] Artha., I. 17.

(agricultural science), gulmavrikshayurveda (botany), Sulabhadhatusastra (metallurgy), and panyavyavahara (trade-regulations). Having thus received necessary training in these professions, people seem to have engaged themselves either in agriculture or industrial works according to their taste. There is evidence to believe that the art of measuring the quantity of rainfall was known[218] and that no agricultural operations were undertaken without ascertaining the quantity of rainfall necessary for the cultivation of various crops.[219] That ancient kings paid special attention and care to agriculture and industry, they being the chief source of revenue to their states is evident from the following humane rules of Kautilya :—

"(1) Lands prepared for cultivation shall be given to taxpayers only for life ; and unprepared lands shall not be taken from those who are preparing them for cultivation.

"(2) Lands may be confiscated from those who do not properly cultivate them.

"(3) The king shall bestow on cultivators material help and remission of taxes and treat with fatherly kindness those who have passed the period of remission of taxes.

"(4) He shall carry on mining operations and manufactures and exploit timber and elephant forests, offering facilities for cattle-breeding and trade, constructing roads for traffic both by land and water, and setting up market towns.

"(5) He shall also construct reservoirs filled with water either perennial or drawn from some other source.

---

218 Artha., II. 5.

219 Artha., II. 24.

"(6) The king shall exercise his right of ownership with regard to fishing, ferrying, and trading in vegetables in reservoirs or lakes.

"(7) Elders among the villagers shall improve the property of bereaved minors till they attain their age; so also the property of gods.

"(8) There shall be in villages no buildings intended for sports and plays. Nor shall actors, dancers, singers and other bands of amusements enter into villages and disturb the villagers from their constant field work.

"(9) The king shall protect agriculture from the molestation of courtiers, of workmen, of robbers, of boundary guards, and of stray cattle.

"(10) He shall set apart pasture grounds for grazing cattle."[220]

Attention has already been drawn to the attempts of ancient kings to colonize waste lands by employing wealthy persons as tributary chiefs or Viceroys over the proposed colony.

Besides agriculture, some industrial undertakings such as mining, exploitation of forests, liquor-manufacture, weaving, cattle-breeding, and coining seem to have been carried on under state supervision also in addition to private enterprise. Though mining, weaving and other industrial operations were undertaken by ancient states as a profitable concern, they seem to have also served the purpose of poor-houses opened for the relief of the poor and the helpless. This is confirmed by the following statement of the Arthasastra (II. 23) :—

"Those women who do not stir out of their houses, those whose husbands are gone abroad, and those who are cripple or girls may, when obliged to work for subsistence,

---

[220] Artha., II. 1 and 2.

be provided with work (spinning out threads with due courtesy through maidservants of the weaving establishment."

In this way ancient kings seem to have relieved themselves of unnecessary expenditure of state-revenue in discharging the obligatory duty of providing for the maintenance of the orphans, the aged, the infirm, and helpless women (Artha., II. 1).

Much doubt is entertained as to the existence of coined money in Vedic India. Satamana,[221] Krishnala[222] Nishka and other Vedic words which in later literature signify coins of specific weight and form are taken to mean weights and ornaments in the Vedas.[223] The table of coins is thus stated in Smriti literature (Smritichandrika, Vol. III, p. 230) :—

	3	Barley corns	=	...	1 Krishnala
	5	Krishnalas	=	...	1 Masha
I	16	Mashas ...	=	...	1 Suvarna
	4	Suvarnas ...	=	...	1 Pala or Nishka
	10	Palas ...	=	...	1 Dharana
	2	Krishnalas	=	...	1 Silver Masha
II	16	Mashas ...	=	...	1 Dharana or purana
	10	Dharanas ...	=	...	1 Silver Sataman or Nishka

III 1 Copper pana or Karshapana = $\frac{1}{4}$ Pala of silver.

There is no doubt that trade in Vedic India was largely carried on by bartering commodities (Rig., IV. 24. 10), settling the price in terms of a cow, taken as a unit of value or Rûpa. In Rigveda VIII. 1, 5 a picture or image of India is offered in sale for ten cows. Still

---

[221] Satapatha, XII. 7, 2, 13 ; 9, 1, 4.

[222] Tai. Br., I. 3, 6, 7.

[223] Vedic Index, Vol. I, pp. 196-97.

there is no reason to deny that in the Vedic period a beginning was made to fix the price of commodities in terms of Krishnalas or Nishkas, as in those of a cow, and pave the way for the introduction of gold and silver currency at a later period. From this it may be inferred that coinage of money was at the outset a mercantile device and became at a later period state monopoly on account of its being a profitable source of revenue to the state in the form of discount and commission and other charges.[224] Whether the art of coining money was Babylonian convention or Indian is a question which I have reserved for future investigation.

Being coeval with division of labour, trade was a social necessity and was carried on with little or no restrictions imposed upon it by kings; or in other words it was free trade. The policy of fair or protective trade came later. As already pointed out, monarchy began with the right to levy a tax on agriculture and trade for the purpose of meeting the necessary expenses of the government. As the machinery of the government became more and more complex, kings began to expand the sources of the revenue by multiplying the number of taxes they had a right to impose on agriculture and trade. Even so far back as the 4th century B. C. politicians seem to have been divided in their opinion as to the desirability of having a free or protective trade policy. The difference of views on this vexed question which even now remains unsettled is thus referred to in the Arthasastra (VIII. 4):—

"My teacher says that of the two, the Superintendent of the boundary and the trader, the former destroys traffic by allowing thieves and taking taxes more than he

[224] Artha., II. 12.

ought to, whereas the trader renders the country prosperous by a favourable barter of commercial articles.

"No, says Kautilya : the Superintendent of the boundary increases traffic by welcoming the arrival of merchandise, whereas traders unite in causing rise and fall in the value of articles, and live by making profits, cent. per cent. in *panas* or Kumbhas (measures of grain)."

Thus Kautilya was not merely a protectionist as opposed to his teacher who was a free-trader, but something more. He seems to have regarded trade as a necessary evil, for he terms traders as thieves (Artha., IV. 1) :—

"Thus traders, artisans, musicians, beggars, buffoons and other idlers who are thieves in effect though not in name shall be restrained from oppression on the country."

Again in IV. 4, he says :—

"There are thirteen kinds of criminals who, secretly attempting to live by foul means, destroy the peace of the country. They shall either be banished or made to pay an adequate compensation according as their guilt is light or serious."

Who formed these thirteen kinds of criminals is very difficult to determine. Among the followers of various professions of bad repute mentioned in the fourth Adhikarana of the Arthasastra, there are about eighteen persons whose movements are said to be closely watched. They are: (1) weavers, (2) washermen, (3) goldsmiths, (4) examiner of coins, (5) scavengers, (6) physicians, (7) musicians, (8) traders, (9) beggars, (10) buffoons, (11) false witnesses, (12) wizards, (13) poisoners, (14) counterfeit coiners, (15) robbers, (16) murderers, (17) judges and clerks given to bribery and (18) debauched persons.

All these eighteen classes have been termed disturbers of public peace (Kantaka); and the precautionary measures to be taken against them have been clearly stated in the 4th book of the Arthasastra. Thus restrictions against the freedom of the people in their agricultural, industrial or commercial pursuits seem to have varied with the nature of the government, they being very few in the republican form of the government that prevailed from the Vedic down to the Kautilya period. It may be asserted without fear of contradiction that subsequent to the Kautilya period, the people of India had to contend against various restrictions against their economical pursuits and that inspite of those restrictions, they had not much disturbance in their enjoyment of plenty and peace. The three essential factors conducive to a nation's plenty, peace and security are the active industrial habits of the people, their religious morality and the government. The first two, industry and religion, act and react upon each other. Honest industry promotes honest religious or moral thinking and the honest and self-denying tenets of a religion such as those of Jainism and Buddhism tend to make the people more contented than profiteering industrial pursuits and help the government in governing the people with little or no friction. It is the pure religious fervour of the people that enabled the kings of the Vedic and Buddhistic periods to commend security within and to concentrate their attention against enemies without. I believe that it is the same religious fervour that has contributed to the preservation of the peace in India during the recent four years' horrible conflagration in Europe.

Laxity in morality and religion produces immoral and licentious proceedings, and renders the government more and more despotic. Thus the decline of Jainism and Buddhism is marked by rise of despotic governments in India, as a self-preserving measure.

APPENDIX A

[225]Election of Kings and Delegation of Sovereignty

Besides the discussion of scientific and sacrificial subjects, political subjects such as land-disputes, criminal complaints, cases of gambling, election of kings, war and peace questions and the like seem to have engaged the attention of the members of the religious and political assembly. From Vaj. S., XX. 17 where the poet prays to be absolved from the sin he and his companions might have committed 'in village or in wild, assembly or corporeal sense, to a Sudra or Aryya or to either's disadvantage,'[226] it appears that the political assembly was guilty of giving wrong judgments in some cases, especially against the Sudras and the agricultural people. As a supreme judicial organ of the state, the assembly seems to have had powers not merely to confiscate the food and other property of a citizen or to expel the head of a family (Taitt. S., III. 4, 8, 5-6) evidently for misconduct, but also to degrade a king to the rank of the common people or of the clan of nobles, as implied in the following passage of the Nidana Sutra (VII. 10) :—

"The sacrifice to be performed for the prosperity of a Vaisya is the next. They say that this is for the prosperity of a Vaisya who, as an ordinary noble, is inclined to attain sovereignty. But Sandilya adds to this the rite of installation with anointment, thinking that this is a sacrifice for the prosperity (restoration) of a noble (râjnah)

---

[225] Maitra S., IV. 7, 4.

[226] *Cf.* Maitra S., I. 10, 2; Chhandogya, V. 36.

who, on account of his reckless foolhardiness and habitual addiction to gambling, has retired."

Also the custom of delegating sovereign power to the Adhvaryu priest for two years during a horse-sacrifice undertaken by ancient kings is a far more reliable evidence that the king was entirely at the mercy of the peoples' assembly and especially of the priestly class. The delegation of royal power to the Adhvaryu priest is thus stated in the Bodhayana Srauta Sutra (XV. 4):—

"Here (in the horse-sacrifice), those who anoint a Kshatra as the king anoint the Adhvaryu (in his stead). He (the Kshatriya king) says—'O Brahmans and princes, the Adhvaryu will be the king these two years; obey him; whoever does not obey him, the whole property of him they will confiscate.' Accordingly the Adhvaryu is the king these two years."

Apastamba (XX. 2, 12; 3, 1-2) also says the same thing, but makes no mention of any penalty for disobedience:—

"He (the king) hands over the kingdom to the Adhvaryu; and says, 'O Brahmans and princes, this Adhvaryu is your king; whatever loyal respect is due to me, the same from you may be shown to him; whatever he does by you (or to you), the same shall be considered as authoritatively done to you. As long as the sacrifice lasts, the Adhvaryu becomes the king."

Confiscation of property seems to have been one of the usual penalties meted out for political offences; for Bodhayana lays down the same punishment to be inflicted on a person who, disregarding the royal proclamation, lets out mares to mingle with the sacrificial horse that is let out to roam about[227] at its will. From the delegation of royal

[227] Bodhayana Srauta, XV. 8.

power to Brahmans it is clear that though the Kshatriyas were created for royal sway and for furnishing soldiers to protect the Iranian and Aryan settlements in India, royalty was not yet considered to be a monopoly of a class or family. There is evidence to believe that this delegation of royal power was prevalent prior to the split between the Devas and the Asuras, inasmuch as one of the sons of Virochana, an Asura king, is said to have performed a horse-sacrifice with Brahman priests.[228]

---

[228] Aitareya Br., VIII. 4, 22.

APPENDIX B.

SACRIFICIAL FASTING AS A FORM OF PASSIVE RESISTANCE

In all the conflicts, whether between man and man, or between the king and his people, or between the king and his sons or wives, one of the most powerful weapon, successfully employed by the weak against the strong, seems to have been the vow of abstinence observed till death or till the removal of the cause of dispute, whichever might happen earlier. This vow is termed Âtma-medha, self-immolation in the Kathaka Sambita and *prâyopareśa* in the epics and other later literary works, and it appears to have originated from the Vedic Vrata or the formal taking of the vow of abstinence, enjoined on all persons that undertake to perform a sacrifice. The day or days when this Vrata is observed are called Upavasatha or fast-days and the number of these fast-days may be one or more according to the intention and capacity of the sacrificer. And in favour of those who are, however, incapable to observe the vow of abstinence in connection with any Vedic rite, an expiatory offering into the fire with the words 'Tvam Agni Ayâsyayâsan,[229] etc.,' is enjoined. It is likely therefore that the observance of the vow of abstinence which forms part of all Vedic sacrifices inclusive of those sacrifices which are enjoined upon a people desirous to install, expel or restore a king or upon a king, desirous to surmount difficulties in collecting taxes from his refractory and turbulent subjects or in

---

[229] Ekagnikanda, I. 5, 18.

commanding obedience from his people, army or kinsmen or restoring order in his own or conquered country was converted as a most useful political weapon within the reach of all. The success or effectiveness of this form of passive resistance or threat depended upon the universal belief of the people of those days that the state, city or the house in which one or more persons, especially Brahmans, whether men or women, are allowed to starve to death either intentionally or otherwise will sooner or later come to ruin, and that those who are the causes of such deaths will be the worst sinners and fall into the hell. This belief is found expressed in the beginning of the Kathopanishad.[230] Here in atonement for the sinful act of allowing Nachiketas to fast for three days in the house of Yama, the king of the departed souls, in his absence, the latter is stated to have given to the former any three boons the guest might choose. The Âtmamedha sacrifice is thus described in the Kathaka Samhita (29, 9):—

"Having created all creatures, Prajapati found himself impoverished. He then discovered the eleven victims and offered them. So whoever finds himself impoverished should nourish himself by offering (the eleven victims). He should offer these eleven victims in any sacrifice. Ten are the vital airs in man, and the soul is the eleventh. With these he nourishes all the constituents of his own being. Agni is made up of all the gods; with Agni's victim all the gods are therefore propitiated. The soul is Agni's victim. Speech is Sarasvati's victim; because it is Sarasvati's victim, he unites speech with the soul, making a couple thereby. Then Soma's victim: Soma is the bearer of the seed;

---

[230] See also Satapatha Brāhmaṇa, II. 1, 4, 2.

verily it is the couple that bears the seed. Then the victim of Pushan: the beasts are such; verily it is Pushan that procreates. Then the victim of Brihaspati: Brahma is Brihaspati; verily Brahma lords over the beasts. Then the victim of all-gods: these people belong to the all-gods; these he unites with Brahma. Then the victim of Indra: the Kshatra or ruling power is Indra; he places the Kshatra in lordship over the people. Then the victim of the Maruts: the clans belong to the Maruts; the clans he unites with the Ruling power. Then the victim of Indra-and-Agni: verily splendour and power are Indra-and-Agni; he unites the clans with the Ruling power through splendour and power. Then Savitri's victim is for procreation. Then Varuna's victim is for liberation. Prajapati under Varuna created all these beings. They all abandoned him and went up. He desired that they should be near him. So he performed a penance: he was about to *sacrifice himself* (âtmanam medhâya âlabhata). Then they approached him and were afraid of him; they bowed down; hence it is that all these beings move about stuck to the earth; they all worshipped him bringing tributes (bali), the earth with sacrificial ground, the herbs with sacred grass, the waters with sprinkling water, the trees with offering sticks and stakes, the sheep and goats with beasts, with curd and ghi the cows; verily the gods are the givers of tributes. Prajapati is no other than sacrifice; to him all these bring tribute. Whoever knows that they bring him tribute (will attain happiness)."

Kathaka S. XXIX. 9.

The meaning of this passage, when divested of its technical obscurities, is this: whoever desires to attain an object surmounting all opposition should undertake the performance of any one of the sacrifices laid down in the Vedas and instead of taking the trouble of procuring the goat and other eleven sacrificial victims appropriate to the eleven gods, Agni, Sarasvân, Soma, Pushan, Brihaspati, the All-gods, Indra, the Maruts, Indra-and-Agni, Savitri, and Varuna, he should sacrifice himself as a fit victim, apparently by fasting, composed as he is of eleven parts, the ten vital airs and the soul, corresponding to the eleven sacrificial victims, after the manner of the Âtma-medha performed by Prajapati when he found himself deserted by the offspring of his own creation. It is taken for granted that his opponents would be terrified and would help him to attain his desired object in the same way as the world did towards Prajapati.

There can be no doubt that the Âtma-medha form of passive resistance was invented by the Vedic poets to check the licentious proceedings of some of their Asura kings. While from Kâthaka, V. 6, where a poet prays wishing plenty of food, people and wealth, wide imperial sway and a good assembly to an Asura king, we are given to understand that there were some good Asura kings, another passage from the same Samhita (XII. 2) describes the Asuras as licentious (Manasvitarâh) and prescribes a sacrifice under the name Sangrahana, capturing, in view of captivating the mind of the Asuras. Besides using self-immolation, the Vedic Aryans seem also to have had recourse to the policy of *divide et impera* by preferring Mitra-worshippers to Varuna-worshippers (Kathaka S., XXI. 10; Maitra S., III. 10) and *vice versâ*, or by honouring Indra more than Varun and *vice versâ* (Taitt. S., VI. 6, 5) in view of replacing in the kingdom a Varuna-worshipper by an Indra-worshipping king, or putting the people against the king[231] and *vice versâ*. This

[231] Maitra S., II. 1, 9; III. 8, 10; Taitt. S., II. 2, 11: Kathaka S., XXI. 10; XXIX. 8.

passive resistance, usually undertaken to defeat an opponent in a civil dispute,[232] to recover a bad debt, or inheritance,[233] to compel a king to change his unjust attitude[234] or to withdraw an unjust imposition,[235] to expel a tyrannical king,[236] minister[237] or official, to put down rebellion of the people against the king,[238] to restore a banished king,[239] to reclaim a king from his wicked habits,[240] to avert premature deaths due to the sinful acts of a king,[241] or to open the eyes of a stubborn opponent to his reckless attitude,[242] or to avert an impending punishment[243] or public slander or contempt, is found resorted to not merely by the weak, but also the strong prior to active retribution.[244] From Rajatarangini VI. 14, it appears that ancient kings used to send spies to find out and report voluntary cases of prâyopaveśa or fasting to death and to redress such grievances as were the causes of these long fasts. It is probable that Kaikeyi's success in her attempt to prevail upon Dasaratha to send Rama in banishment and instal Bharata, her own son, in his place, is due to her threat of committing suicide by starvation. There can be no doubt that in those far off days when men sincerely shuddered at the mere thought of

---

232 Taitt. S., II. 2, 3.

233 Artha Sastra, V. 1 (p. 298 Trans.); Taitt. S., III. 1, 9.

234 A. V., V. 18.

235 A. V., III. 29. 586.

236 & 238 Taitt. S., II. 3, 1; III. 4, 8; Rajatarangini, V. 468.

237 A. V., VII. 94.

239 A. V., I. 29.

240 The story of Asamanjaso, son of Sagara.

241 *Vide* the story of Sambhuka in Ramayana.

242 Ramayana Yuddhakanda, Chap. 21.

243 *Ibid*, Kishkindhakanda, Chap. 55.

244 *Cf.* Rajatarangini, IV. 82, 99; V. 468; VI. 25, 336, 343; VII. 13, 1088, 1157, 1611; VIII. 51, 110, 656, 709, 768, 808, 937, 2224, 2733, 2739.

their being the cause of human death by starvation, the prâyopaveśa form of passive resistance proved a most effective weapon in the hand of the weak and the oppressed against their wicked oppressors, and that that power was also misused on a number of occasions. But with the advance of science and scientific religious thoughts the sentimental basis and handle of this effective weapon have long been shattered, and blown to the wind and the resumption of this form of passive resistance in the name of Satyagraha now is nothing but a suicidal attempt at rebuilding a ruined castle on a sandy ground with no solid foundation to stand on. Equally useless seems to be the refusal on the part of the people to pay taxes and supply men for the army as much as the same form of resistance on the part of the people, on the one hand, and the attempt on the part of the king's officers to put down the resistance, on the other, seem to have occasioned much bloodshed even in those far-off days of Kautilya.[245]

---

[245] Arthasastra, V. 1.

APPENDIX C

STATE-OWNERSHIP OF LAND

One of the most interesting of the fundamental political principles that deserves our attention here is the question relating to king's or emperor's right of ownership of land and man. This is an important question that has long been exercising the minds of statesmen and politicians all the world over and has not yet been definitely settled. The question is whether an emperor or his feudal chief can justly claim and exercise his right of ownership over the land and men in his empire or state. This has been answered in two different ways. The Mîmânsakas or the school of the Vedic exegetics headed by Jaimini hold that neither an emperor (Sârvabhauma) nor a feudal chief (Mândalika) is justified in exercising any right of ownership over the state land or his people, whether father, mother or children or his servants. They say that he is only entitled to a fixed share of revenue in kind in virtue of his protective care and that the land and other natural things of the state are common to all. This is the conclusion arrived at by Jaimini and his commentators who have discussed the point in all its bearings (Mimansaka Sutras, VI. 7, 2).

Quite opposed to this is the view held by Kautilya, the author of the Arthasâstra. He says for example, that the king shall exercise his right of ownership with regard to fishing, ferrying, and trading in vegetables in reservoirs or lakes (II..1); that besides collecting revenue, the king shall keep as a state monopoly both mining and commerce

(II. 12) ; and in view of justifying the levy of an extra water-tax (II. 24) his commentator, Bhattasvâmi, quotes a verse in which the state-ownership of land and water is clearly mentioned. The verse runs as follows :—

"Those who are well versed in the Sastras admit that the king is the owner of both land and water and that the people can only exercise their right of ownership over all other things except these two." (P. 144, Eng. Trans.)

The view that is held by the Mimansakas seems to be the view that is still current in the transactions of the villagers in India : whenever they sell a piece of land, they declare in the bond the transfer of eight kinds of enjoyment, such as (1) nidhi (treasure-trove), (2) nikshepa (deposit hidden in the earth), (3) water, (4) trees, (5) stones, (6) âgâmi, anything that may come in future, (7) sanchita, anything that is standing, and (8) Akshina, imperishable. This declaration is evidently opposed to the view held by Kautilya and other later politicians who held that any treasure-trove contained in the earth, any deposit of money and the like concealed in the earth, and salt and other minerals together with water are what the king alone can justly claim as his property.

As the Mimânsaka view of land-tenure is in agreement not merely with the history of social evolution all the world over, but also with the nature of the political constitution which obtained in India during the Vedic and the Brâhmanic periods, the historical importance of Jaimini's view on this question cannot be overvalued. Hence I add here below my own translation of the Sutras of Jaimini together with their commentaries by Pârthasârathi Misra :

The sutras (VI. 7, 2) are thus commented upon by Pârthasârathi Misra :—

It is declared in the Vedas that in the Visvajit sacrifice the sacrificer makes a gift of all that is his own. There as to the doubt whether even the cognates that are designated by the word 'sva,' 'one's own,' are to be given over or only such wealth as he can claim to be his own, it may be asserted that in the absence of particularisation, all that is implied by the word 'sva,' one's own, should be given over; for it is possible to render father and others subservient to others; the act of bringing a thing under the ownership of another man is what is meant by a gift, hence father and others should also be given over.—But it is not so; evidently they cannot be made over as a gift, in as much as a gift in the real sense of the word means 'the relinquishing of one's ownership of a thing and the placing of it under the ownership of another'; accordingly (a father cannot be given over), for a father cannot become no-father, though he is given over. But only that which can be called one's own in virtue of his exercising his right of lordship over it can be given over as a gift; for, when such a thing is gifted, the original owner gets rid of his ownership and the donee acquires it. Also the word 'sva,' 'one's own,' means in virtue of its diverse significant power 'self,' 'one's own,' 'cognates,' and 'wealth.' Of these several meanings, it means a single particular meaning in a particular context. Since among the meanings it is only wealth that forms a proper article of gift, the word 'sva' is here used only in that sense. Hence only wealth, but not father and others.

As to the question whether that which is the broad earth should be gifted or not, the holder of the *primâ facie* view speaks of it as an article of gift, thinking that it is the wealth of the emperor. But this is no one's property (sva). Consisting as it does in the protection of, and the removal of the wicked from, his state, sovereignty (râjya) means the collection of taxes from the agriculturists and others and of fines from the guilty (dandya); this much is the relation (between the king and his state), but no lordship or ownership (svamitva). Hence no emperor shall make a gift of the broad earth, nor a feudal chief his feudal land.

As to the doubt, whether a Sûdra who attends upon a master as his servant in view of doing the religious duty should be given over as a gift or not, it may be said that he should be given over, in as much as it is inclusively favoured by the epithet "all" and also it is possible to render him subservient to another. But as there is no master's ownership with reference to him and as there is the possibility of dislike on his part to accept subserviency to another, he should not be given over.—But a slave (dâsa) may after all be given over as a gift.

In the seventh discourse of his Vivada-bhangarnava,[246] Jagannatha Tarkapanchanana agrees with the Mimansakas in the view that the king is no owner of the land and is entitled only to certain amount of tax on it, the cultivator of the land being by time-honoured custom its real owner with right of alienation. The context in which he states this view is the sale of a slave girl by one of many brothers, in the house of each of whom she is made to work in turn, as agreed upon during the time of the division of inheritance. The slave woman is compared to the land which may change hands by sale. The translation of the text is as follows :—

Brihaspati says that a single woman should be made to work in each house (*i.e.*, the house of each of the brothers) according to the share of inheritance.—Well, there arises a doubt here whether the slave woman should or should not go to work on the appointed days in the houses of other brothers, if she is sold to a stranger by one of the brothers

[246] A 284, Manuscript, Government Oriental Library, Mysore.

on the day when she had to work in the seller's house—we reply thus : the purchaser has acquired the same kind of property right in her that the seller had in her before selling. Hence the purchaser has right to command her service only for as many days as she attended on her seller by turns in the middle of each month. It is also for this reason that in the kingdom (country) purchased by a king, his right of possession of the country extends only to the collection of taxes on it ; and at the same time there remains the right of ownership vested in the cultivator, in virtue of which he is entitled to the produce. Hence also the claim of a cultivator who cultivates a piece of land and enjoys the produce after paying taxes due to the king, to its ownership is admitted on all hands. Hence it is that when the owner of the land sells the land, the purchaser acquires the same right of ownership in virtue of which he is entitled to its enjoyment after paying the taxes due to the king ; and that the cultivator's ownership of the land is never denied, as such denial is quite opposed to custom (vyavahāra). Accordingly since various kinds of ownership with regard to a single property are accepted, it must be presumed that claims of two different persons to the same kind of ownership with regard to a property are opposed to each other.